Wc

A

**48 Hiking Tracks
on Twenty Islands**

Graf Editions

Using this book

This book was conceived as a compact pictorial walking guide. Several innovative ideas have been included for easier orientation on your treks:

AWT stands for **Actual Walking Time**. This does not include breaks, wrong turnings, sight-seeing or anything of a similar nature. The AWT serves as a personal control as to whether certain route markings, emphasised in **bold print** in the book, have been reached in the given time. If not, you have gone wrong somewhere. These times are not aimed at achieving a record performance, but are individual components of the tour.

The approximate **overall length** of a walk is specified in hours in the introduction of each tour. These figures do not incorporate time taken for bus journeys or extra-long breaks.

Route photos are intended for your own orientation purposes, for consulting locals and as a stimulus. They have been taken at different times of the year and can be found as figs. **1** to **8** in the texts.

The **route sketches** have been drawn to the best of our knowledge, though do not lay claim to completeness.

The author Dieter Graf is a widely travelled architect. The Aegean has been his preferred hiking destination for many years during which time he has been witness to great change.
For this book he spent many months on the Cyclades and can count himself as a connoisseur of the islands.

©2000 Graf Editions, Munich, Germany
All rights reserved.

Original title: Wandern auf den Kykladen
English translation: Sally Darlington, München
Design: Rudolf Paulus Gorbach, Buchendorf
Maps: Kurt Zucher, Starnberg
Cover photo: Dietrich Gehl, Stuttgart

ISBN 3-9803130-5-0

Contents

The Cyclades

You have chosen one of the most beautiful regions of Europe as your destination. Regardless whether you spend your time in fixed hotel accommodation, island hopping or sailing to different places, in order to fully understand the Cyclades you should explore them on foot filling your five senses with the scent of thyme, the clatter of sheep bells, the sight of small field chapels and the feel of field walls, not forgetting the taste of retsina on your tongue during the midday rest under an olive tree, this being one of the most intensive hiking experiences. Leave everything behind you for a few hours and wander through the loneliness of a Cycladic island.

Landscape

The Cyclades form the peaks of an underwater mountain range which sank during the Tertiary period and whose "valleys" lie 200 metres or more below sea level. The islands in the north are mainly composed of marble, granite, gneiss and schist, whereas Mílos and Santoríni are partly of volcanic origin. To the south, where the European and African continental plates collide, volcanic eruptions and earthquakes occur such as that on Santoríni and Anáfi in 1956.

In antiquity, the existing forests were already being felled for ship building or were ravaged by summer forest fires with the result that today, particularly on higher ground, a karst-type landscape exists. Only on valley floors and skilfully erected hillside terraces is it possible to practice agriculture. In many cases it became impossible to feed the population from the meagre harvests causing many island-ers to emigrate to the mainland, though also to America and Australia.

The vegetation on the Cyclades differs widely. Andros, Naxos, Paros, Sífnos and Tínos are greener than the other islands. Shady trees on trekking routes are rare, making them all the more valuable as resting places. There are Aleppo pines, huge mulberry trees, ancient chestnut oaks and cypresses in cemeteries, poplars, planes and dappled eucalyptus trees on avenues and squares, tamarisks on the beaches and olive trees which take on a bizarre gnarled appearance with age. Other trees bear pomegranates, cherries, figs, walnuts, almonds, oranges and lemons. In the scrub, known as phrýgana in Greece, we find agaves, prickly pears, broom, oleander and hibiscus as well as all sorts of kitchen herbs.

The list of fauna on the Cyclades, other than the domesticated varieties, is short: rabbits, lizards (which rustle in passing), tortoises, frogs and little else. Snakes are seldom seen as they disappear instantly without a sound at the first tremor. Large snakes are usually harmless. The poisonous sand viper is similar to an adder and grows up to 50 cm. It's bite can be lethal. There are also scorpions, though their painful bites are not fatal.

History

The name Cyclades comes from ancient times and signifies that the archipelago forms a kyklos, or ring, around the sacred island of Delos.

Their position between Europe and Asia made the Cyclades a bridge between the two cultures and one of the oldest landscapes in Europe to be cultivated by man from a very early age. The first immigrants, the Carians, came from Asia Minor. As early as 6,000 years ago, 3,500 years prior to advanced Greek civilisation, stone idols, which count among the sources of art of the Mycenaen period, were carved.

Following the arrival of the Dorians from the north around 1100 BC, the Cyclades became part of Greece with Delos as its intellectual and cultural centre. Here was the nucleus of the Athenian-Delian League, the protective alliance against Persia, which bound the Greeks of the Aegean and Asia Minor with Athens. The final victory of the Greeks over the Persians in 449 BC kept the Asian conquerors from invading the Mediterranean for 2000 years. Immense riches were amassed on Delos during the Golden Age which followed. When Athens carried off the treasure and tried to make vassals of its allies, the islands fought against Athens in allegiance with Sparta in the Peloponnesian War.

The outcome was a forever weakened Greece which fell under the rule of Macedonia in 339 BC. The Macedonian, Alexander the Great, carried Greek culture, henceforth known as "Hellenic", for a short period to India. Having made Greek culture their own, the Romans, as the later rulers, helped its spread throughout Europe after 146 BC. The Greek culture had become that of the Occident.

Christianity also became the state religion of the Eastern Roman Empire, still known as Byzantium, after 391 AD. Following the fall of the Western Roman Empire in 476 AD during the migration of peoples, the eastern part of the Imperium Romanum remained an upholder of Graeco-Roman culture. Byzantium, the second Rome, missionized the Slavs and spread Greek ideas as far as Moscow, which later become known as the Second Byzantium or Third Rome. However, Europe began to drift apart in cultural

terms and religious differences also deepened. In 1054 the schism or final separation of the Eastern Greek-Orthodox Church from the Western Latin Church of Rome reached a climax.

In the meantime, in the wake of the Persians, Avars, Arabs and Seljuks, a new great Asian power had assembled on the eastern borders of Byzantium: the Turkish Ottoman Empire. It pushed westward with immense force. One of the most short-sighted campaigns in history was then initiated. Owing to the good trade relations of Byzantium with Asia and the silk road, rival Venice induced the Crusaders to conquer the capital Constantinople in 1204. The Cyclades came under the rule of Venetian nobility. Though more decisive for Greek culture was the weakening of the power of Byzantium, finally leading to its conquest by the Turks in 1453. Byzantium, the shield behind which Europe had been able to develop, was shattered. Constantinople became Stambul; the cathedral of Hagia Sophia a mosque. The Great Ottoman Empire embarked on the conquest of Europe, penetrating as far as Vienna and Malta.

The advanced Greek civilisation of the Middle Ages no longer flourished. Learned Byzantine fugitives brought Greek thinking with them to the West, paving the way for the Renaissance. Yet the whole of Greek life, from music to diet, was dominated by Turkish influence for the next 350 years. This is still recognisable to a degree today. Only on Tínos were the Venetians able to hold out longer and Síros had a special status by virtue of French protection. Finally, at the outset of the 19th century, Europe reflected on its cultural roots. The political stability of post-Napoleonic Europe and Classicism in art increased awareness of the East. Philhellenists from many countries supported the Greek struggle for independence after 1821 and Greece became a part of Europe again.

120 years later, Mussolini tried in vain with German aid to incorporate Greece into his new Imperium Romanum. With Western help, post World War II Greece avoided the Communist fate of the other Balkan countries and, today, at the dawn of the new millennium, is an enthusiastic member of the new European order.

Trekking

Depending on preference, the best time for hiking is between Greek Easter and October.

Those wanting a feast for the eyes should walk around the Easter period. It can still be somewhat cool and wet, but the islands are green, dotted by red poppies and yellow broom and the houses and alleyways are in the process of being white-washed. The preparations for the Greek Easter celebrations are worth a visit in themselves! However, it is still too cold to swim and some tourist facilities are still closed.

In the low season in May and June, some plants have already lost their bloom, but it is the best time for trekking as there are still only a few tourists. As of the end of May, the sea reaches a pleasant temperature.

The main tourist season in July and August is not necessarily the best period for hiking owing to the heat. But thanks to the meltémi, a northerly, occasionally stormy, wind, walking is still possible, perhaps with a longer midday break under an olive tree. The Church festivals on August 15 (Lady Day) are worth seeing.

In the autumn, from September to mid October, the sea is still ideal for bathing and the heat has become bearable again. This is also a very good time for walking.

From the beginning of October, bars and hotels gradually begin to close. There usually follows a change in the weather from mid October bringing rain. Then it becomes unpleasant.

Hiking maps as we know them do not exist in Greece. Better maps are only available on Amorgós, Folégandros, Naxos, Santoríni and Sífnos. Anyone requiring good maps can purchase (rather expensive) ones on a scale of 1 : 50 000 (printed around 1990) from the Army Survey Office in Athens. It is situated directly north of Areos Park at No. 4, Evelpidon in the YIS (Yeografikí Ipiresía Stratú) in a barracks. Open mornings only, an I.D. is required!

Perhaps it will strike you that the same place names crop up time and again on the maps and that there are different spellings for each name. The highest peak of almost every Cycladic island is named after St. Elias, the weathermaker and successor of the sun god Helios and almost all the churches and chapels on the coast are dedicated to the patron saint of seafarers, St. Nicholas.

According to the ancient Greeks: "Nothing is more enduring than change". This is especially true of the old mule tracks, the monopátia, which have now in fact become superfluous, as the islanders use the asphalt, concrete and dirt roads that have sprung up everywhere. The Greeks meet trekking with a lack of understanding. If you ask someone the way, it is better to ask for the "monopáti", or you'll end up on a road! The uncontrolled urban spread, particularly on Santoríni and Mykonos, has produced a corresponding, frequently exaggerated road development. On Mykonos a track I discovered one day had been concreted over the next. Unfortunately, the same effort in the laying, routing and replanting of new roads is not used as in the building of new houses in accordance with the strict regulations of the "Cycladic style".

Some of what one encounters on treks does not, therefore, meet everyone's sense of order or the environmental regulations back home. When it comes to refuse, some Greeks remain true to themselves: they are uninhibited. Great street cleaning efforts are put to a severe test by the population. As rubbish avoidance is hardly practised, one sometimes comes across large, smoking refuse dumps.

The routes described have been retraced shortly before going to print and can be readily followed with a normal level of fitness; no particular surety of foot is required. Short cuts have been added in the longer treks. All the starting and finishing points are served by public busses, even in the low season. To appreciate the views, the hikes usually lead from the mountains to the sea – so don't forget your swimming gear.

Anther tip: donkey manure is a safer pointer as to a path than goat droppings, as goat tracks generally end somewhere on pasture land.

Naturally no liability can be assumed for accidents, for civil-law demands from property owners, departure or opening times or the suchlike.

Adequate hiking equipment should include a day-pack, shoes with good soles, long trousers (or zipped trousers for the scrub), possibly binoculars and a mobile phone, a whistle and picnic provisions as well as a rain garment, where required, in the spring and autumn. An adapter and earplugs (cockerels) with you for your hotel might come in handy. A smattering of Greek should be part of your mental equipment:

ágios, agía, AG – *saint*	órmos – *bay*
apano – *up, upwards*	Panagía – *Mother of God*
aristerá – *left*	panigíri – *parish fair*
caldéra – *caldera*	papás – *Greek priest*
chóra – *main village*	parakaló – *please*
chorió – *village*	parélia – *harbour road*
dexiá – *right*	pigí – *spring*
drómos – *road*	platía – *square*
efcharistó – *thank you*	pósso káni aftó? –
endáxi – *okay*	*how much is it?*
ikonostase – *altar screen*	psomí – *bread*
ísia – *straight ahead*	puíne? – *where is?*
jassas – *hello*	posin óra? – *how long?*
kástro – *Venetian castle*	pyrgos – *fortified tower*
káto – *downwards*	skála – *stone stairway*
ksoklísi – *rural chapel*	sto kaló – *all the best*
langádgi – *gorge, ravine*	thálassa – *sea*
moní – *monastery*	tirí – *cheese*
monopáti – *path*	wounó – *mountain*
ne/óchi – *yes/no*	xinolithía – *dry-stone wall*
nero – *water*	phrýgana – *scrub, the enemy*
óra – *hour*	*of the Cycladic hiker*

Amorgós

Amorgós is a very mountainous and comparatively barren island. In some places rugged cliff faces of schist and limestone drop steeply into the sea. Some old mountain villages have been able to maintain their original appearance. They are linked by ancient monopátia, some of which have been widened to dirt tracks. A good map (by Dr. Georg Perreiter, 1 : 50 000) can be bought anywhere on the island.

Ancient Arkesíni ④

❶ The Bay of Egiali

*On this five-hour tour offering beautiful
views we hike through rich vegetation.
It can get hot in the valley basin above
Egiali in the summer and there are no
tavernas for four hours.*

AWT 0.00   We set off from the **village square** next to the bus stop in
Langáda on a downhill track towards the mountains. The
track ❶ is concrete but is still delightful. The view to the
left overlooks Tholária and some ruins in the valley. We
continue straight on ahead on a slight incline through
0.10   fields with vines, cacti and olive trees up to a **blue signpost** which points up right to the attractive paved stone
footpath ❷. Fig trees line the gentle uphill path. After a
0.25   **ditch** (dry bed) the way is stepped before becoming a well-
trodden rocky path. When the high corner of a wall bars
the way, we bear left and continue on below a tunnel of
0.45   trees. Near a **chapel** ❸ the monastery suddenly comes into
view. The route below the monastery leads towards a wall
where it forks.

> *Alternative:* the right fork (sign) leads to Stavrós
> Monastery below Mt. Kríkelo, the highest peak on
> Amorgós, in an hour.

0.55   We climb up left towards the monastery of **Agios Ioannis
Theologios.**

> *The monastery shelters from the meltémi behind a hill and
> faces south onto the monastery fields. It is abandoned and
> shines only outwardly in its former glory. There are some
> fresco remains in the apse within, but they are in very poor
> repair. The room however, consisting of a dome with a
> barrel roof in front, is of very fine proportions.*

On the plateau above the monastery courtyard, our main
interest is the hollow to the west in which there lies a rect-
angular stable. We reach it without a trail through a labyrinth of walls going downhill (dusty red path) until we
1.10   reach a **wall** which closes off the entire valley. A fence runs
two metres parallel to it. To the left of the valley centre we
come across a stony monopáti ❹ which leads down to the
blue dome of the Epanochori Church.

We first have to pass through a wire gate whose closing
mechanism requires a certain degree of technical under-

standing. The stony track heads further on down to the lower
1.20 **gate**, to the right of which are several stables. Here the track widens and trees provide shady picnic spots with a superb Cycladic view.

At the bottom the path veers left,
1.30 runs through a **dry bed**, and becomes a rugged scree path ◱ before joining onto the original concrete track. We turn right to the
1.45 church of **Panagia Epanochori** (abbreviated as Panachoriani).

> *Here is everything you need: a cistern behind the church, shady cypresses with steps to sit on in front of the church, bread and tomatoes in the backpack.*
> **Short cut:** if you have had

enough of idyllic Greek hiking, you can return to Langáda in 15 minutes by taking the concrete track and then descending on a shady gravel path beneath olive trees to the beach in 30 minutes. There are two routes leading down to swim.

But the gourmets among us plan a wonderful panorama route: the cement track turns into a path below the church. This leads around the flank of the hill which hides the sea from view. After the bend the bay comes into sight again, as does the slope up to Tholária ◱, half way up the moun-
1.55 tain. We take a right turn at the **fork** above the incline, past the chapel of Ag. Taxiarchis, facing the bay of Aiyiali / Ägiáli / Ejáli / Egiali (all correct) the whole time.
2.25 Some steps lead up to **Tholária** ◱. Here there are tavernas and busses to the valley.

The dirt track down to the sea commences directly below the square near the bus station and Hotel Vigla. We ignore the first monopáti which soon forks downhill to the left.
2.30 Our track widens and is paved. At the **fork**, we stroll down the left turning beneath olive trees, past a rural chapel ◱. In the plain below we bear left, drawing an arc and, after a dry bed, arrive on a roadway and turn right. Past the petrol station, left at the asphalt road, the first track right

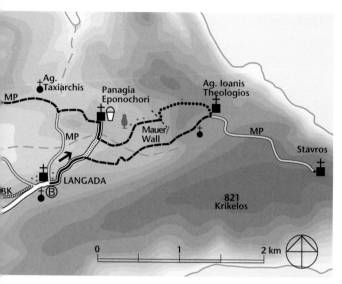

2.55 and we are on the **beach.** And two minutes later in the water! Afterwards we'll take a drink of course, perhaps in the dreamy garden tavern "Lakki".

The busses leave Ormos Egiali rather seldom in the late afternoon. Though it is pleasant waiting in the tavernas. Route length: approx. eight kilometres.

Eponochori

② High Above Katápola

Katápola means "lower town", which once stood for ancient Minóa and now for Chóra. We intend to visit both places by foot in five to six hours. We first climb the extremely attractive mule track to the main village of the island, continue almost horizontally to the abandoned convent of Valsamitís and descend towards the excavation sites of Minóa before turning back to Katápola. There are several springs en route, but tavernas only in Amorgós town.

AWT 0.00   Our route begins in **Katápola-Xilókeratídi**, at Katharinaís "Moon Bar". It is pleasant to sit and have a coffee under the shady tamarisk **1** – if it is already open. From the café we take the charming alley up on the left to St. George's Hotel and then turn right. We reach the fields at a chapel (left). The path leads into the valley, half way up whose right flank our trail will later climb. It is lined by olive trees and grain fields **2**. You should keep over to the right on the valley floor in order to find the gravel road which winds its way through the valley. Above right on the slope, outside the built-up area, is a barrel-roofed chapel and, 200 m further on, some ruins. Keep them in view! Our roadway leads further into the valley on the flat. Some 50 m left of

0.20   the **ruins** we ascend the monopáti **3** up to the foothills of the mountain. At the top you suddenly realise how elegantly we have skirted the refuse site of Katápola! In the right bend of the dirt road take the marked path leading up left and you'll reach the old way to Chóra. This

★   storybook path **4** lies partly in the shadow of olive trees.
0.35   Below left in the valley is a **chapel**, and en route you'll find "Water for drink" in a cistern. Then head towards a wall –
0.50   and up the steps on the right. We soon see the first **houses**
1.00   **5** and the fort and, below the bus part, arrive in **Chóra**. You stroll through the small town up to the main square **6**, turn right before reaching the church and soon come to the post office. At the telephone box (… maybe phone home, ask how the weather is?) bear right, then right again down a gentle slope. As a house bars the way, you take a left and then first right and thus reach a concrete ramp at

1.10   the end of the village leading to the **road.** A footpath 30 m on the left leads downhill. Turn left at the crossing below and then down left again at a house. For a while we walk over bare rock in a ditch; above right is the torso of a windmill.

Two chapels slumber on the slope to the right and, at a good distance, the rock of Minóa awaits us. We follow the terraces on a level trail. After the bend we see a chapel with a farmhouse on the opposite slope of a wide valley, carry

1.40   on downhill, come across a **spring** after the hollow at the bottom, then climb up again. Here it is legitimate to crush the plants underfoot as the path is somewhat overgrown.

1.55   After the ridge we take the field track on the left to the **road** and bear right along it for about a kilometre. To the left is the wide, open sea – the Cyclades end here.

To the right of the junction we see the small convent, a chapel above it and, right at the top, the ruins of a Venetian watchtower **7**. We head down the road to the 200 year

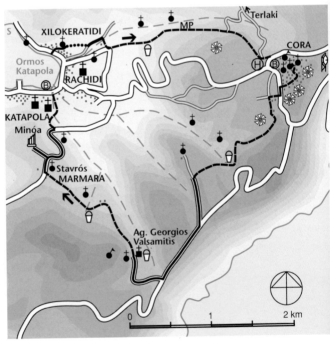

2.10 old, abandoned **Convent of Valsamitís**. The numerous ponds which fed the gardens are still intact and are still maintained today. Time to unpack a leisurely lunch in the shade of the building ...

We leave the convent the same way, going right along the wall and, back in the gardens beneath the tall water-drawing facility, find a beaten path leading across the slope. At the next mountain ledge is a farm and, behind the gully containing a spring, a chapel **8**. We stroll leisurely down to the Marmara saddle and then up again to the Chapel of the Cross. From here we then turn left (sign-

2.55 post) to the excavation site of **Minóa**.

*In recent years enormous progress has been made in the excavation work under the supervision of the resolute professor of archaeology, Ms. Marangou. You now find good descriptions of the Graeco-Roman city. (See also **4**).*

Back at Stavrós/Chapel of the Cross, we take the roadway down on the left and, after the ledge and the right bend,

3.10 should take care not to miss the pretty footpath to **Katápola**! Route length: approx. ten kilometres.

❸ The Monastery High Above the Sea

A round tour of four hours on paths which are sometimes difficult to find around the Profitis Elias to the Monastery of Chosoviótissa. Take something to cover your legs when visiting the monastery and begin your trek at around 10 a.m. You'll need a fairly good head for heights at AWT 2.00 and provisions!

AWT 0.00   We depart from the **aerial mast** above **Chóra**. A track lined by walls leads up left past the aerial mast to the main road which we leave again on the right after 60 m. Here there

0.05   is a walled **concrete track** ❶ which is later paved with stone. After five minutes we pass a gate and the attractive path becomes increasingly difficult to find. We are aided by red circular markings and cairns, but also by the stones

0.20   reddened with kicked-up dust. We soon reach a **walled field** and pass it on the right. Above the field we bear right uphill and then immediately left again. There is a great view of Katápola on the way ahead which leads up to and then under the old electricity line. This then runs about 50 m above on our right.

0.30   Below left is a small **aerial system**. The keen eye of the Cycladic hiker is required so as not to lose the way. Green arrows now point up to the right – but we follow the *red* dots *straight ahead*.

0.40   You arrive at a **plateau** on the mountain ridge. Now keeping a little to the right, we take a path some 20 m left of the rock. The path continues between the road and the electricity lines above ❷. Another ridge has to be passed before turning up to the masts, under the electricity lines

0.50   and down again. Below left are remains of a **windmill** ❸. We remain at this height in a north-easterly direction. The mountain trail now runs below the electricity lines through prickly scrub and is thus easier to recognise. The island of Nikouria lies below us to the left, Donoussa behind it, Naxos to the left in the distance and Koufonisia to the fore. Having come around the mountain, we then see a dirt road ❹ on the right above the asphalt road. This

1.20   is our direction! The roadway leads us to a **saddle** where there is a crossing. A new dirt road has been cut into the slope with unbelievable indifference, partially destroying

the old mountain trail. You continue along this road for about 400 m until you come across the old track which runs parallel, 50 to 70 m below. Glad to leave this monstrosity and having found a safe way down, we wander contentedly along the old mule track high above the sea. Beneath an overhang above is a Panagía chapel. A solitary boulder **5** marks the way which has almost been covered over by the new roadway. This ends abruptly – a new holiday house is probably in the planning.

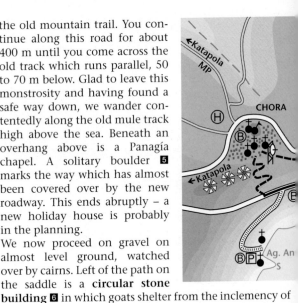

We now proceed on gravel on almost level ground, watched over by cairns. Left of the path on

1.55 the saddle is a **circular stone building** **6** in which goats shelter from the inclemency of the weather. If you take a closer look at the rock ahead, you see something white glistening! After carefully crossing a patch of rubble **7** you may now need a bit of a head for heights. But the path is about a metre wide for a few steps so that you can keep over to the mountain. You then reach an iron-barred door which forms the limits of the monastery grounds. The building itself is not yet in view. We still have to descend a steep path to the left before sighting

2.15 the fortress-like **Chosoviótissa Monastery** **8** and its cistern.

> *The monastery is closed from 13.00 to 17.00 hours and can be visited by both men and women. Those who dislike borrowing clothing should bring along garments to cover their arms and legs. Despite its fortified appearance, the monastery was raided by pirates several times since its foundation in the 9th century. Not only is the breathtakingly beautiful site of the monastery impressive, but so too is the harmonisation of nature and human construction, especially in the interior of the monastery where the rock and the building form the stairway jointly.*
>
> *Visitors are offered small refreshments for which they gladly place a small donation in the alms box.*

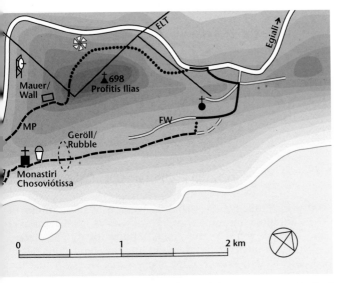

Our tour now continues, along with numerous motorised visitors, downhill over a ramp. The asphalt road begins at the car park which **forks** after 200 m.

2.30

> *Short cut:* there is also a bus stop at the fork for those who have had enough for the day. It was six to seven kilometres after all.
>
> *Alternative:* left, you go down to the small rocky **beach of Agia Anna** in ten minutes. Two chapels, no taverna, a bus stop.

An old trail winds its way up right 400 m behind the car park. To the left you see Astipalea and, behind an overhang to the south, Anáfi. Having reached the top, we pass among aerials and windmill mounds to arrive back in **Chóra**, after eight kilometres.

2.50

❹ Arkesíni

A rather demanding circuit of seven to eight hours to the archaeological sites of Minóa and ancient Arkesíni. We set out on the new dirt road which has been built over the old footpath. A part of the old path still exists, but is now partly overgrown. We continue along attractive monopátia, past a place to bathe, to Kamarí. Here it is possible to stop and eat, then take the bus back. (Ask for the departure times in the morning!)

AWT 0.00 This attractive old island route starts at the **harbour of Katápola** (meaning "lower town" – of Minóa!), leads over uneven steps to the domed church of Ag. Nikolaous, continuing on stone flags out into the countryside. There is a chapel on the slope above – but we reach first the new dirt road which covers the old mule track before turning up right to the Chapel of the Cross (Stavros) on the Marmara saddle ■, occasionally catching sight of the old stone surface shining through. We turn off right at

0.20 the **signpost** and are soon among the ruins of Minóa.

In the 4th millennium BC there was a late Neolithic settlement on the summit, as is documented by a wealth of finds (i.a. Cycladic statuettes). As of the 11th century BC an important town existed here. The earlier assumption that

0.25 ***Minóa** was founded by the Minoans no longer seems tenable. Only buildings from the classical Greek and Roman eras have been discovered so far. Even the layman can recognise the accurately shaped corners of the cyclopean stonework and an ancient torso which once faced in the direction of the next part of our route.*

Road construction on the opposite slope has progressed well – three dirt roads can be seen. We will take the lowest. (The top one is mentioned at the end.*) Looking right across the third bay, we see a chapel – today's destination. To the right, the rocks of classical Arkesíni are distinguishable.

We return to the dirt road and bear right. After 100 m (50 m *before* the fork), next to the farmhouse, the old, practically overgrown monopáti to Léfkes branches off right

downhill between two dry-stone walls. The adventurous among us can continue along this old track, the rest taking 0.40 the gently sloping roadway to **Léfkes** ❷.

We turn left in Léfkes and can relax our limbs on the dirt road. For emergencies there are two cisterns bearing a typical Greek sign. At the hamlet of Ag. Thekla ❸ we happily take leave of the roadway and arrive very shortly 1.00 down in the deserted **bay** of Sarandes. Here flowers await us in the spring, two chapels ❹ ❺ and our only bathing opportunity for today. A high-pitched whine fills the air of this wonderful place.

We climb up pleasant steps and a path ❻ edged to one side. 1.35 There is a farm on the **pass**; we bear left beyond it (below the farm) into a second valley (blue dots). Opposite us, and now closer, is the rock of Arkesíni. On the slope opposite, the path winds again steeply and, on top, there is another farm (to the right). The rather desolate hamlet of Kamari, then the village of Wrustis, with its domed church, and, on a hill to the right, an unusual chapel with a diagonal wall (p. 8) come into sight on the plateau. After passing a dilapidated stable, we head towards the chapel mentioned above, without a path for a while, and then on to 2.00 **Wrustis/Vroutsi** with the tall church of Spyrídon. There is nothing of particular note here. Only the marked trail starting 2.25 here down to the rock of **ancient Arkenísi** (p. 13) is of any significance for us.

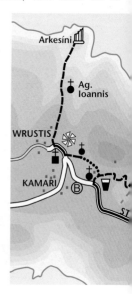

The small Church of St. Mary on the huge chalk cliff first catches our attention. It is assumed that there was a temple to Aphrodite on this site in ancient times. Further down we find town walls built into the rock. The ensemble was founded more than 3000 years ago.

Ahead there is a rock ❼, perfect for a classical picnic, with Naxos as our neighbour. But we should not forget the long return journey!

Back to Wrutsis, past the "leaning" chapel again, bearing right uphill past the stable – up to the road and the
3.00 **chapel with four vaults.** In the café opposite we can debate whether or not to return on foot.

> *Short cut:* from Kamari an afternoon bus returns to Chóra/Katápalo.

Otherwise there is the asphalt road (4 km). Quick progress is made here and then a farmhouse (Stavros) looms ahead – again with a chapel with four vaults **8**. Another five minutes uphill along the road and you find yourself on a
3.55 **small plateau** with an electricity mast, at which three cables meet. (Presumably the broken down VW van will be here for some time to come).

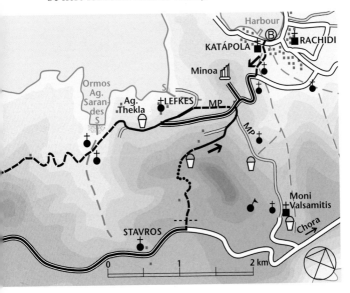

Here we leave the road, bearing left, and pass through a gap in a wall into a high valley with a farmhouse at its centre. We pass it on the right, go through a meadow gate

4.15 again to climb up without a trail onto the **saddle**. Here we have a good view: Léfkes and Minóa lie below us. Another wonderful mountain trail and, immediately after, a spring with a small pool to the right in the rocks! Our fatigue disappears rapidly.

Immediately below us is a house – and the entrance leading up to it. We recognise the kilometre-long track* (for a single house!) from Minóa. But being rather weary, we are indulgent this evening. We sail on down to Minóa and

5.00 then to **Katápola**; at the end on the same way we came. At the harbour, we raise a glass to today's 19 km.

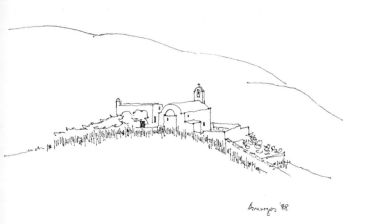

Amorgós '88

Anáfi

The isolated, mountainous, most south-easterly island of the Cyclades is composed of gneiss, quartzite, marble, mica schist and sandstone which have been thrust to the surface by the collision of the European and African continental plates. During the earthquake of 1956, the delightful hilltop site of the chóra of Anáfi experienced the same fate as that of Santoríni. Although sufficient water is available, the island is barely cultivated apart from the odd field of crops on valley floors and protected hollows. It remained largely uninhabited for some 200 years due to marauding pirates which hindered a long rural tradition of path construction.

Chora

⑤ The Marble Rock of Kálamos

This 19 km long trek with a tiring ascent takes eight hours. From May to September it is possible to cover one leg of the journey in a kaiki by sea in half an hour and take in an extended swim. The route leads along the coast for the most part and passes several cisterns and a taverna. There are several very attractive, partly empty beaches for swimming. Unfortunately, a road is planned from Chóra to the monastery. Hopefully the bulldozers will spare this route. So come soon!

AWT 0.00 We follow the route description of the other trek up to the double chapel (AWT 0.12).

> **Short cut:** if you want to save 10 min. and take a more well-beaten track, continue down the road for about 100 m up to the metal signs and turn left onto the main track along the coast. This path joins the path described below at AWT 0.50

0.12 We pass the **double chapel** (p. 37 **1**) on our *left* and take the dirt trail around the mountain. Further below we come across one of the few monopátia on the island. When it "peters out" later on, continue along slightly downhill trails, using the dry bed **1** at the end. At the cistern at the

0.50 end of the gorge, we cross the hollow and, below a chapel, reach the deserted houses of Ag. Erini and the **main track**, turning left down it. You soon see the marble rock of Kálamos **2**, our destination on this trek. Keep left in the valley dotted with oleander bushes, or you will end up in

1.00 the taverna in **Roukonas** – better save it for later!

A steep-sided valley reveals holiday houses next to a mini-windmill with gaily turning sails **3**. The path continues up steeply above the sea and there is soon a whole series of sandy coves ahead and a large monastery above **4**. Having passed the monastery gardens, you end up in front of a locked gate – if you haven't announced your arrival from Chóra.

2.05 *The abandoned **Monastery of Zoodóchos Pigís**, the "life-giving source", is 200 years old and was built on the antique ruins of an Apollo temple **5**. Recycling, so to*

speak. This temple has its origins in the realm of Greek legend. The Argonauts, who stole the Golden Fleece from the "Eldorado" of Colchis on the east coast of the Black Sea, reached Greek land here after a stormy sea journey and set up an altar in gratitude on the site which became a temple in historical times.

The route to the summit next leads past a semi-ancient chicken enclosure, before becoming an easily identifiable rocky path up the mountain ridge. A good head for heights will be needed at the top as steep inclines **6** have to be overcome before we can enjoy the view from the summit, from **Panagía Kalamiótissa**, the patron saint of the island, to well beyond Crete; visibility often only extends as far as the island of Pacheiá, Greek for "the fat one". The summit church was rebuilt after having been destroyed during the tremendous earthquake of 1956. Several churches have been rebuilt several times over the last 400 years. Monks are also supposed to have lived here earlier. Up until a bad accident caused by lightning some 100 years ago, the Anáphians trekked up here for the church celebrations each year! Today they only march up to the monastery on the mountain below. Once the road has been built, the pilgrims' way will be even easier.

3.05

The attractive site of the monastery **7** on the way down may remind some of the descent from Mount Sinai to the Monastery of St. Catherine.

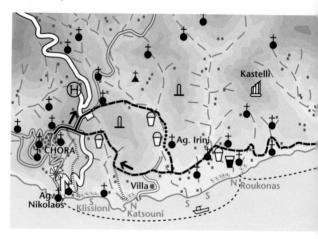

3.55 We return the same way, past the **monastery**. (Or is Jorgo perhaps waiting with his "kalamiótissa" at the mole for the journey back?) In the monastery gardens below, we stop to take some refreshing spring water with us. Later on, when stone, man-high markings (p. 37) appear on the

5.00 left, we descend to the beach and taverna of **Roukonas**. Fortified and refreshed, we turn inland to the main track, pass by Ag. Erini again and then proceed uphill above an

6.00 attractive holiday domicile towards **Chóra**.

Alternative: at the holiday house you could go in the direction of **Ag. Nikólaos** towards Klissioni and then continue on to the harbour.

▶ From **Chóra** to the **beach of Klissioni**. A trail from the last guest-house at the end of the village below the road leads to two chapels and then down the hill opposite Chóra to the road. After a short stretch you reach the road leading to Klissioni (see map).

▶ To reach the **beach of Katsouni** follow the road to the harbour for about 500 m and, at the signs to Kastélli, turn left onto a path, then right again downhill (see map).

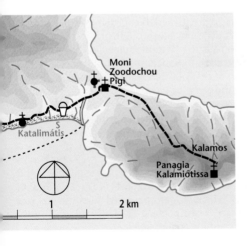

⑥ Ancient Anáphe

This six-hour, rather exhausting hilly circuit leads to the remains of the ancient town of Anáphe and then on down to the sandy beach of Roukonas, where you can stop at a tavern. You arrive back in Chóra along narrow paths above the coast.
Water and perhaps food should be taken along as the cisterns at midway do not inspire much confidence. If you intend to return by boat, you should ask for the times in the morning.

AWT 0.00 From **Chóra** you take the road leading downhill, turn up left after 350 m onto an asphalt track and then bear right down to the gravel/lime works. Above the plant there is a

0.12 monopáti leading up left towards a **double chapel** ❶. You pass it on the left and soon find yourself on an attractive sunken path leading downhill. At the end of the valley you come past an olive grove and a farmhouse with a traditional oven. You go round the agaves in the valley, then turn up right at the fork to the hilltop and head up through

0.30 a hollow between two **houses** ❷. You turn right at the top then bear up left at the fork. There is a house on the hill to the right which you pass by in a wide arc. After a small pass there is a green hollow below right and, behind it, a wide mountain ridge with a marker post in the middle. You

0.45 soon reach a **saddle** (❸, arrow), left of the ridge, along trails. Opposite us is the Kastélli mountain to the right of whose peak once lay the ancient town of Anáphe ❹. We meander down over mountain trails, keeping left at first, then more to the right to where two valleys meet and a

0.55 small farmhouse stands ❺. Next to the house on the **valley floor** we find a small garden with vines, lemons and pomegranates.

Having proceeded a few steps up the right of the two valleys, we take the trail leading up right opposite a commemorative cross. The path runs on past some ruins and

1.15 a stable up a slight incline to the **chapel of Docari Panagía** ❻, in front of which a well-preserved sarcophagus has found its present resting place ❼. Griffons, the horse Pegasus and six cupids are depicted.

1.25 *After a ten-minute climb, we are now right of the summit among the few remains of the **Dorian town of Anáphe**, built around 800 BC. It was abandoned after Roman times, about 500 AD, probably after an earthquake. At the time a processional road led from here to the temple of Apollo in Kálamos. Up to 1998, exquisite marble statues from the Roman period were found on the site. They were partly damaged in a clearing fire and are now on display at the museum in Chóra. There are only a few relics, including a water container, still "in situ".*

We head down towards the sea without a path. On the left we see tall, ancient cairns on a rock above the sea **8**. They acted as signals for ships which were pulled onto land at the landing in Anáphe below. On the site today is the
1.50 Robinson beach of **Roukonas** and a taverna.

At the western end of the beach, to the left of the dry valley, are several paths which run along the coast to a large
2.10 **holiday villa** (p. 33 **8**) from where a wide track leads uphill. (If you go left at the villa fence, you come to the bay of Klissioni.) At the fork at the top, we take the wide
2.45 path left to **Chóra**.

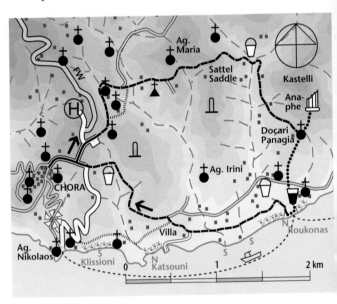

Ándros

The northernmost of the Cycladic islands forms a
link with the Greek mainland, both in terms of
architecture as well as vegetation: the sloped
tiled roofs and the landscape characterised by an
intensive green dotted with cypress trees and
scattered houses are rather reminiscent of Italy. It
is divided by four ranges of schist mountains
with fertile valleys between them.
This large island with its plentiful water supply is
ideally suited for hiking as many mule tracks are
still intact as a result of intensive cultivation.

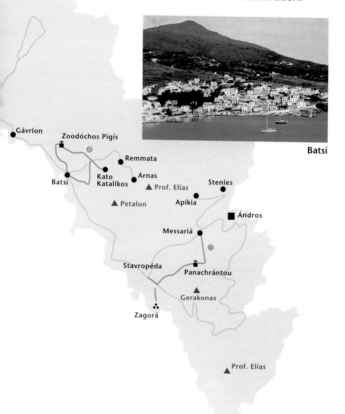

Batsí

⑦ Andros' Monastery

This beautiful trek is well sign-posted at first and leads through a green, cultivated valley and then steeply uphill to the monastery of Panachrántou. From here you wander below the mountain through the fields heading west. This tour of 10 km takes five hours and there are no tavernas en route. It is advisable to find out the bus times before from Stavropéda or order a taxi (Tel. 4 10 81). A short cut can be taken from the monastery.

You take the bus to **Messariá-Taxiarchis**, the bus stop furthest east. Culture buffs can take a quick look at the exterior of the famous, but unfortunately rather dilapidated Byzantine Church of the Archangel. (Sign: Taxiarchis).

AWT 0.00 Our way continues on the road above, obliquely opposite the attractive terraced tavern "**Dionysos**" (unfortunately open evenings only) on to the sign-posted path. Although concrete at the outset, it soon turns out to be one of the most beautiful Cyladic trails of all. Having crossed the bypass further down, you soon find yourself among olive

★ trees and fields **1**. Small red and white metal signs bearing a "1" guide us safely, in Alpine mountaineering club manner, through the landscape. Past a ravine with a waterfall and deep rocky pools on the left. Across a medieval

0.18 **bridge 2** and up into a cross valley with the monastery and the village of Falíka **3** perched up above. The gradient becomes steeper up the opposite slope to the top of the ridge. From here we follow the route markings at a wide

0.35 right bend. Bear left at the two **wooden signs** until you meet some wide steps and the town of Andros is below you

1.15 on the left. We soon reach the fortified **monastery of Panachrántou.**

The 900 year-old monastery housed up to 400 monks in the past. Today there are five, after the monk Eftókimos had "held the fort" alone for decades. Visitors are welcome to enter, see the chapel and have something sweet in the friendly reception room. You should take your time in the church, letting yourself be shown the icon of Panagía Panachántou and the skull of St. Pandelímou.

Short cut: you can reach Falíka by taking the dirt track from below the monastery. First you descend the steps to the right after the church, finding an attractive way in the valley basin back to the route signs. (AWT 0.35).

1.15 Opposite the entrance steps is the monastery *garage,* to the right of which a level trail begins below the rock **4**, later running down between two walls. The right-hand wall serves to guide us safely: it leads us straight downhill to a wall running at a right angle to it, which you go along to the left. The walls stand close together, offering shade, and lead on over level ground. Through a dry bed, following the contour lines, you turn right at the fork, still level, and

2.00 then later down an incline to **Orinó**. In the village we see the church on our right and follow the concrete track left. This leads us out of Orino **6** onto a field track which soon

2.20 forks. Turning left, we reach the hamlet of **Achadó** lying in a hollow.

Trekkers keep an eye out: some 250 m after the hollow, you see a new house to the right on the way up. This leads onto the old monopáti lying to the right below the roadway! Red dot! (If you miss it, you will end up in the village of Zaganiaris). A rural chapel **7** appearing soon in a field confirms you are on the correct, attractive, rather overgrown path through the fields **8**, which follows the contour lines towards the sea.

2.35 After a shady hollow, you pass beneath the **high-voltage power line** which runs from the mainland to Mykonos. Then on through another two dry beds, the second being more of a "sewage bed". Here you turn right past some

2.55 ruins to the **road** and then right again up to the crossing

3.00 known as **Stavropéda**. The busses wait here, provided you are on time.

> *Time and energy left? Then on to the ancient town of* ***Zagoras!*** *At exactly AWT 2.55, is the chapel of Ag. Triada, behind which you bear left and then down right. You first see some ruins, followed by a chapel on the right. It takes 25 min. along the beautiful route above the dramatic formations of the rocky coastline to the defence wall of the ruined town from Geometric times (800 BC).*
>
> *It is recommendable to do the excursion to Zagoras on another day and to visit the archaeological museum in Chóra beforehand.*

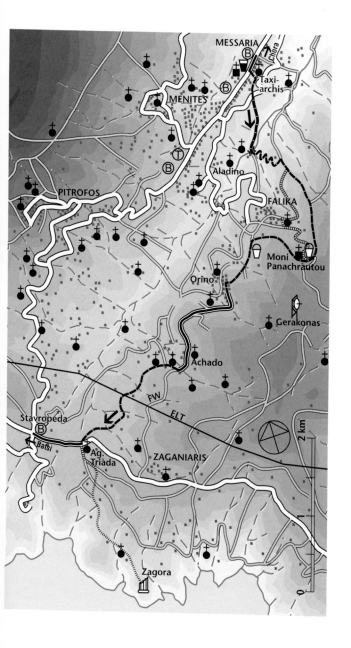

⑧ Andros' Convent

This five hour tour first leads along attractive mule tracks from Batsí to the mighty Convent of Zoodóchos Pigís, and then on through a fertile valley to the village of Katákilos. It is advisable to inquire whether the garden tavernas are open. We return along wonderful hillside trails back to Batsí.

AWT 0.00 From the middle of **Batsí** beach, right of Hotel Glani, we head inland on the concrete road, bear left after the cinema and, further up, left again up a steep slope. Then along a trail and up some steps before swiftly crossing the bypass onto the dirt track opposite. We carry on uphill past the next two forks. About 100 m after the second, in a right bend with some ruins, we find the old monopáti on the left above, offering a fabulous view over Batsí **1**. Unfortu-

0.20 nately, the **dirt road** catches up with us again. It leads to a house with a fence behind which we turn down left, then right to a hidden chapel **2**. From the shaded forecourt some steps lined with sage lead down to an attractive spring with a marble basin. A few metres further on, after the drinking trough, we continue up a mule track on the right. As it later becomes somewhat overgrown, it is better to walk above the path over the open ground – do not follow the left wall downhill!! The wall comes back up and then runs to the left of our footpath, the latter bearing all the charm of the Cyclades **3**. Next, at a row of cypress trees

1.00 **4** we head right uphill to the **road** leading to the convent.

*The 700 year old **Convent of Zoodóchos Pigís**, "Agías" for short, was reopened in 1928 as a convent. It had housed up to 1000 monks in earlier days. A church with a magnificent iconostasis stands in the centre of the inner courtyard, flanked by meagre living quarters towards the valley and by a mighty defence wall above. The "life-giving" source, which gave the convent its name, is in front of the church. Visitors should ring the bell before 11 a.m. and then may only perhaps be allowed in.*

The road continues uphill between the convent and the chapel. On past the closed east face of the convent **5** we

1.15 reach a **crossing** at a cistern and turn left. 100m after the

high-tension power line down right. On the other side of the valley we see the scattered village of Katálikos. Heading downhill, we aim towards the second pylon, turn right along the wall in front of it and then down over open ground onto a **roadway** which leads us left. At the fork below next to a few house ruins, we proceed downhill to the right towards the valley floor and then back up to the **asphalt road.**

1.40

2.10

> *If you want to go to Kato Katalikos, the road leading down left, then left again into the valley below with the shady terraced taverns gets you there in 10 min. If they are open you could take a taxi back …*

2.10 The way back to Batsí begins next to this road, uphill to the right on a dirt track. After approx. 300 m you see a wide, somewhat overgrown roadway on the right. Continuing along it, we soon reach a mule track leading around the slope **6** (blue markings). It makes a wide left bend into a green valley **7** with a staggered crossing. We

★   go straight on, past a deserted house, between delightful

2.35 terraces of olive trees **8** and turn right at the **fork** in front of the high-tension power line. At the fork *after* a spring, the red dot points us down right into the valley. We turn

2.50 left at the **road**, then right downhill along the concrete

3.00 path to the **harbour of Batsí.**

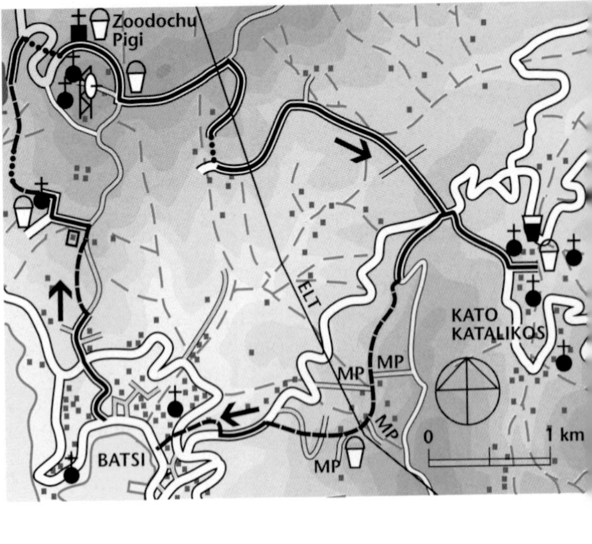

Donoússa

The most northerly and remote of the "Small Cyclades" is very mountainous and practically treeless. Geologically, it is composed of marble, quartzite and schist. Unfortunately a vehicle track has largely destroyed the former mule track leading around the island. The route described here runs along parallel paths, thus making an attractive tour of the island possible again.

⑨ Tour of the Island

The five to six hour trek begins with an innocuous climb to about 250 m and a descent to the wide bay of Kalotarítissa. After a short climb, we take a horizontal route right round the island. There are cisterns on the way – but no tavernas.

AWT

0.00 We depart from below the **village church** of Timios Stavros, heading northwards. Past the schools we reach a dirt road, cross the track, leaving the "windmill" behind us on the left, and climb slowly up a mule track to the left of a dry bed. After crossing it, the path climbs gently until

0.45 we reach a windy **pass** below Mt. Papás. Looking down over the protected bay (fig.), along past the cliffs, we turn

1.10 down left to the unspoilt hamlet of **Kalotarítissa.**
We head on along a monopáti whose days are very probably numbered. It still leads us leisurely along the coast and then uphill – until we meet the unsealed road. An eight-metre (!) wide monstrosity has been carved into the landscape. Absurd for the handful of cars on the island.
The old monopáti lies buried under it. Later, in a right-hand bend, when a fence comes into view down below to the left, one can flee from this monstrosity and reach

2.10 **Mersíni** without a path by going left across the terraces. Having taken the steep concrete path downhill in Mersíni, you see a round, rusty German naval mine to your right,

leaning peacefully against a wall in the sun, and arrive at
2.15 a **spring** five minutes later. The water splashes wondrously
beneath the huge acorn tree throughout the year.

Turning back a few metres, you now head left above the
solar collectors until you meet a path leading down left.
Keeping to the right, you arrive in the often deserted sandy
2.30 bay of **Livádi** and feel like Robinson Crusoe.

On the opposite side, at the cairn, you continue uphill
along a trail and then, higher up, without a path to the
2.55 round **stump of a windmill.** If you trudge on inland going
downhill from here, you soon find a monopáti leading to
the wide dirt road. You take the left bend of the road at the
cleft in the valley (water culvert), taking care not to overlook the narrow way which heads up after 50 m on the
right. This takes you to the upper part of the hamlet of
3.05 **Messaría** and, at the next fork, straight on and then down
into the valley. Here you cross the dirt road and follow
the dry bed towards Kéntros beach for 50 m before taking
what is left of the old path up on the right. Proceed another
80 m along the road and then up right after the electricity
cables to the double church of Panagía, and, from here,
3.40 down to **Stavros.** Approx. 10 km.

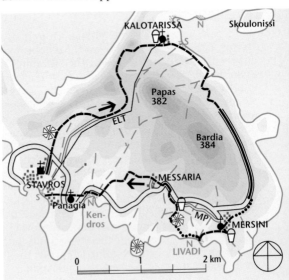

Folégandros

This island exposed to a stormy climate is composed of marble in the east and schist in the west. The eastern part is only cultivated to a small extent and is very barren, whereas the terraces for crops in the west are still worked. Here, in particular, it is possible to hike along old mule tracks. A good Greek map of the island by DEMO on a scale of 1 : 25 000 can be obtained anywhere.

Chora

⑩ Folégandros' Western Beaches

This trek along the sandy beaches of Angáli and Ag. Nikolaos to the village of Áno Meriá shows the charming side of Folégandros. Easily identifiable monopátia lead through terraced fields and gardens. Shady taverns await us on the beaches.

AWT 0.00 The **footpath ❶** makes its way from below the north-western edge of the beautiful chóra, high above the sea and the terraces, and below the road. Following the contour lines, it leads on to the flat-topped chapel on the pass and
0.12 then **❷** at a sharp angle to the **road**, along which we proceed to the next pass (cleft in the terrain) before turning left 50 m after the chapel onto the monopáti above. This mule track, with only one wall on the left, leads to a
0.20 **hollow ❸** above which is the only farmhouse in the area. The paved trail leads back up and is then walled on both sides. When the walls drift apart, we follow the one on the right downhill in a wide arc. Then comes a big surprise: the trail in this mountainous area is suddenly paved with multicoloured marble slabs. An olive grove becomes vis-
★ ible above the sea and a chapel completes this delightful Cycladic picture **❹**. The idyll ends 150 m below the
0.30 **chapel**, however, and you have to take sheep tracks down towards a solitary house. Below the house to the right is
0.40 a stony **bay**. From here you reach the sandy beach of
0.50 **Angáli ❺** along small paths which wind their way through the rocks. You are not always alone here, as boats bring bathers to the beach during the season.

Alternative: from Angáli back to **Chóra**.

1. Express route: directly above the beach to the right is a dry bed, which looks like a wide dirt track. Head up to the right of it for 150 m. Now go right, keeping 20 m above the dry bed and then, after about 8 minutes in the narrowing valley, bear up to the right along a narrow, somewhat overgrown mule track, almost up to the road. Turn right here onto the foot-path which forks to the left from the way you came. (40 minutes).

2. Panorama route: from the beach, walk about 550 m along a dirt road lined with oleanders until you come

to a cistern (left). Directly opposite, a roadway swings up right to a house. At the top go straight ahead along the mule track below the house and then along the slope up to the road. Continue as above (45 minutes).
3. *Modern route:* head up the dirt track to the road and wait there for the bus. (Usually takes longest).

0.50 **From Angáli straight to Áno Meriá**

You take the dirt road which leads away from the beach for about 550 m up to the cistern (left). After another 20 m, you find a narrow, hidden way heading up on the left, which leads to a wide, flat path around the hill. After approx. 200 m, you turn off right onto an attractive, rubble path **7** up a steep incline to Áno Meriá. Some lizards basking in the evening sun, dart away with a rustle. Now and again we come across a farmer from Áno Meriá, who greets in a friendly manner and casts a worried look at our hiker's legs. Looking back, we see across the entire island and down to the bay of Angáli **8** below. There is a cistern on the left. Here we head straight ahead onto the road and

1.25   then, further up, into the long, drawn-out village of **Áno Meriá**. You can wait for the bus in the general store/kafeneion with the friendly owner.

0.50   **From Angáli via Ag. Nikolaos to Àno Meriá**

1.05   A path leads directly above the sea to the tamarisk-lined pebble bay of **Ag. Nikolaos** ⬛. Here we find a panoramic café and holidaying Robinsons under the trees. The bathers are therefore more or less naked.

From behind the beach house, the way leads through a gap in the wall and then later uphill (red dots). The walls narrow at a cleft, placing us between them, and then continue uphill onto a monopáti. Going up along a gradual

1.20   incline, we reach a **crossing** ahead of some ruins. Choosing the uphill fork, we then pass above the Museum of Ethnology (open from 5 p.m.) along to the bus stop of

1.45   **Áno Meriá.**

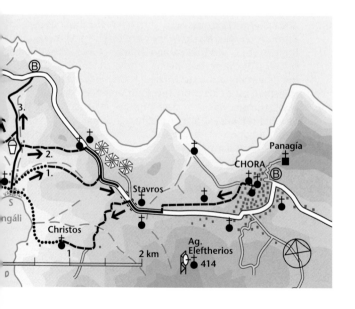

⑪ Folégandros' Eastern Beaches

In three hours from Chóra over dirt tracks and stony paths to the harbour of Karavostássis. A seven km trek through a karstic landscape, along paths which are rocky at times though easy to find.
There are several beaches to choose from, but taverns only in Karavostássis.

AWT 0.00 From the southern fringe of **Chóra**, we come to the bypass at the **petrol station.** We follow this right, taking a sharp left after 80 m onto a concrete path lined by walls on both sides ❶. This runs along the bottom of a slope past some houses, several of which are ruins. At the fork (heliport),

0.12 we proceed on the flat and reach a **saddle** ❷ from where we see a large hollow and, in the distance, the hamlet of Petroussis. The hollow is barely cultivated – a typically karst-type Cycladic landscape. It's hard to imagine that there was a large tree population here 2000 years ago!

August 20: it is not so empty here today. Heavily armed men in camouflage patrol on mopeds and in cars. The hunting season has begun.

0.35 100 m **below Petroussis**, we turn left behind an olive grove onto a monopáti ❸. Up to the right on the next mountain, Profitis Elias, a barrel-roofed chapel shines like a lighthouse. The route becomes a stony, downhill path, still lined by walls at the start. These soon peter out and we use the small church up on the right and the shot cartridge cases thrown away by the hunters as orientation. The Prophet remains above us to the right. The path ❹ is now rather rocky and somewhat arduous to walk along. A village lies at the foot of the Prophet. The way there is easy to find, becoming wider and reddish in colour. Having

1.05 arrived in the barren hamlet of **Livádi**, we soon reach the sea ❻ by turning left downhill at the fork.

Alternative: to the beach of **Katergo.** Turn right at the fork onto the well-trodden path, up the hill past some house ruins and down a steep incline from there to the beach ❺. For the detour you will need 60 minutes there and back. There isn't a safe way along the coast over to the beach of Livádi! Katergo beach is usually empty apart from the few visitors who come here by

boat to swim. On the way back, you can use a reddish dry valley below Livádi as a short cut.

There is a wide dirt track leading from Livádi to the rather
1.25 desolate **beach 7** of the same name. The road then takes
1.40 us past several small beaches and on to **Karavostássis 8**. Here you can wait for the bus in one of several tavernas or swim at one of the two local beaches.

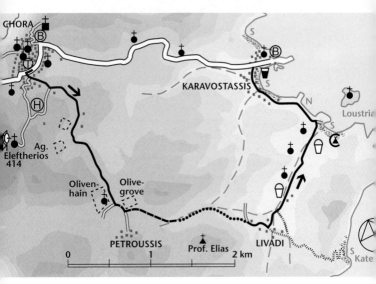

Ios

Schist, marble and gneiss are the rocks of which this island is composed. Since the scarcity of water only allows for a limited degree of agriculture, tourism has provided a very welcome source of income since the sixties. Despite the sun&surf image of this "hippy" island, one can still find very attractive, peaceful trails, especially in the interior of the island.

⑫ Two Sandy Beaches

A circular trek of three and a half to four hours from an overcrowded beach to a lonely one. The first part of the route leads through cleft valleys without a trail, making orientation a little difficult. We use old mule tracks for the way back. There are no tavernas or cisterns en route. Long trousers are recommended.

You take the **bus** from Chóra to the wide, busy, sandy bay of **Mylopótas** ❶ and get off at the last stop. Here we go up

AWT 0.00   left from the **hotel "Gorgona"**. Behind the houses we look for a way up. The mountain top with the TV mast should remain on our left. At the beginning it is best to take a trail ❷ some 80 m from the sea and gain height later on, as there is an impassable ditch on the shore below. We reach a saddle and come across strange retaining walls which look like stone benches. Now we should bear left uphill as it

0.15   becomes flatter above. Having crossed some **wall remains**, we can already see our destination in the distance – a small, sandy beach ❸. After passing around and down the hill, we come to a plain with the remains of a settlement. An

0.20   accurately **laid-out threshing** ❹ circle is still well preserved. Now continue along a path, half way up, before heading on between grandiose rocks and then turning down into a ditch. On the other side of a dry bed (red dots), we proceed up a steep incline through thorny phrýgana. It is best to stay about 150 m below the summit. What looked like a refuse dump from the other side, fortunately

0.35   turns out to be numerous white **marble rocks:** we can best continue at this height. Once around the mountain ridge, we have a better view of the sandy bay and the house ❺. We have to scramble down over the bizarre, rocky coast; later on, we follow the remains of a path in the ditch below. The valley is now fenced off in front of a house, but there is a way through at the water's edge. We overcome the last hurdle with the aid of the pole, and have now reached the

0.55   sandy bay of **Sapounochoma**. White arrows leading around the private house mark the way; here one doesn't disturb the guests.

Now for a rest!

The way back begins behind the house and leads uphill under the electricity wires. It is marked with white dots and has a thick cover of vegetation. 50 m below the electricity cable, which runs parallel to the slope, there is an old path 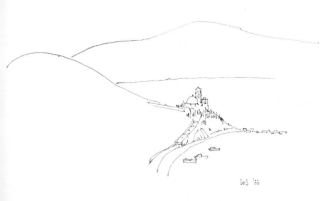❻ onto which we turn left and then once again enjoy the view down to "our" bay and over towards Síkinos. Vertical stone slabs direct us like crash-barriers through the maze of rocks. The path disappears after a narrow pass ❼, but we spot a trail of sorts on the opposite slope – here we turn up right from the top (red dots), can

1.30   see Chóra again and join onto a **dirt road** straight away, which we follow for 50 m before turning off right. Having gone over the pass and under the electricity wires, we notice a wide, old mule track, 80 m to the east. It leads us into the valley.

We are soon presented with a rather strong picture of contrasts – our old island trail above and the loud tourist attractions ❽ below. We come back onto the moped track which we leave again by turning right 150 m after the fork. A wide rock is discernible on the right below which we can use as a path. Soon we are back in the holiday world of

1.50   **Mylopótas.**

Ios Ίος

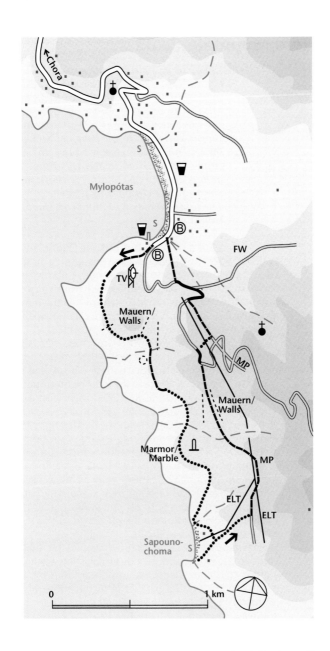

Chora

S

Mylopótas

S

B

B

FW

TV

Mauern/
Walls

MP

Mauern/
Walls

Marmor/
Marble

MP

ELT

ELT

Sapouno-
choma

S

0   1 km

⑬ Two Mountain Peaks

In five to six hours we hike gently uphill below Profitis Elias, the second highest mountain on the island, to the highest one, Mt. Pírgos, and then either back along the same attractive path to Chóra or over thorns and rocks to the beach of Mylopótas for a swim. In any case, we have an enjoyable break on the terrace of the monastery of Agios Ioánnis with its superb views of the neighbouring islands.
The fakirs among us can hike in short trousers.

AWT 0.00 We head uphill past the **windmills of Chóra**, very soon realising why they were built on this particular site, and then follow the signs to the "Odysseus Elytis Theatre". Some steps soon lead straight uphill from the concrete road to the first chapel (right). Behind it is the new open-air theatre, built tastefully into the landscape in the ancient manner – tourism makes it possible.

0.10 Wonderful steps lead up further and then, *after* the **third chapel ❶**, the path forks. We bear right and are soon completely alone on our attractive path ❷. Ahead of us lies our goal, Mt. Pírgos and, above to the left, the mountain of the Prophet Elias, one with a mast, the other with a chapel. The path winds down to a hollow ❸ and, as it is overgrown at times, it is better to walk above it. At a right fork, we continue straight ahead over wide slabs of rock down to a

0.40 **cleft** dotted with oleander bushes which is green even in summer. From here we see Mt. Elias behind us and, further up right, a few houses with an unsurfaced road below. At least we are not entirely alone! The path then suddenly disappears: only the masts ❹ are still there to guide us. After continuing up left ahead of the rock (red dots), the going gets difficult.

Several worn trails lead uphill towards the masts. We come to the saddle and see a dirt road, some beehives and a green cleft below left. It is now an arduous job finding paths which climb up parallel to it, but soon we see the monastery ❺ high on the left. Don't cross the ravine until you reach the top! Rampant heather covers every inch of

1.45   the way, but somehow we make it to the **Monastery of Ágios Ioánnis** .

> *Not a bad place! From the terrace we can see Profitis Elias below us, the protector of seafarers between Síkinos and Antiparos/Paros* ◻. *Naxos, the Small Cyclades and half of Amorgós lie to the north. A temple is said to have stood here in antiquity; understandable with this view.*
>
> *We draw the water for our lunch from the large tap in the monastery courtyard. Stone benches and tables dominate the monastery grounds, the locked chapel receding into the background. During the Panigíri, the parish festival on June 20, food and dance seem to be the most important things. Our two terrace tables have been reserved for 35 people. Hopefully they won't all come today!*

There are two different ways to continue from here. The descent to the beach of Mylopótas is arduous. Anyone looking for an easy way home, should take the same way back – with a different direction of view.

Otherwise we climb up to the next pass, reaching **Mt.**

2.00   **Pírgos** (714 m) along a rough road. Here you have a really superb view over to Santoríni but are otherwise surrounded by rugged countryside and the hum of technology. We head down again on the

2.15   off-road stretch up to a **fork.** The reservoir is visible below ◻, as is a small chapel next to the dirt track. Bearing downhill over some rocks in this direction, we cross a green valley before coming across the

2.35   flat-roofed **chapel.**

> ***Alternative:*** *you can go right along the dirt road and then later wander down the path we came up (see map ALT).*

We cross the dirt road at the chapel, heading west towards the open sea, and later come across some ruins. Their interiors give us an idea of the frugal life of those days – little wonder that the younger generation has emigrated. We now climb up hill and down dale, towards Elias, and then up to

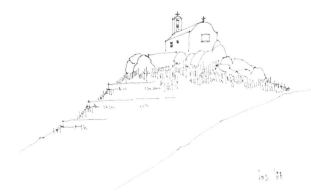

the mountain ledge. Everything is overgrown – and we
search for a way over to the olive trees on a hill above the
site where the valleys meet. Once there, we wind our way
down over crumbling terraces, head through a stream and
3.10   a chicken-coop to the **reservoir** of Mylopótas and on to
3.30   the **sea.** First we go in for a swim before returning to Chóra
on the shuttle bus!

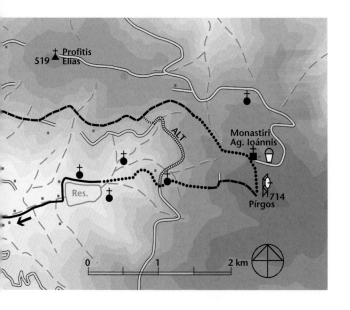

Iráklia

You still find the charm of earlier Cycladic sojourns on this mountainous island. It is well suited for hiking as some of the old mule tracks have survived and are still in use. A map of the island can be bought from the tavern "Perigiali".

⑭ The Cave of St. John

This five-hour trek leads to the famous cave of St. John below Mt. Papás, the highest mountain on the island. The return journey takes us via Panagía, in reality the main village on the island. One can't necessarily rely on the tavernas being open here in the low season. When visiting the cave you should take a torch or candles or, at least, a lighter with you.

AWT

0.00   We leave the village starting from the **Taxiarchis Church** at the top end of the village along a roadway.

0.13   At the second **fork** you bear *right* onto a narrow path which soon becomes a trail. We are guided by a wall to the left, soon joined by another on the right: the monopáti is now whole again and we can turn our attention back to the view. Below the hamlet you continue straight ahead and, just before it, after the gate, climb the last few metres on

0.40   the old monopáti up to **Ágios Athanássis**.
Having walked through the group of three modest houses, you reach a gate after the third house and then another monopáti leading to a ditch. On the other side you go uphill following the route markings and keeping slightly

1.05   to the left. At the top of the **ridge** you go through an opening in the wall. Head on downhill for a while without a trail until you see a clear path above the bay leading

1.30   around the mountain, directly to the cave of **Ag. Ioánnis**.
On the left is the large cave chamber where the big church festival takes place on August 29 for which the entire population of the island gathers. On the right is a small

cave with a bell in front of it (fig.). If you light a few of the candles around the altar inside, you can perhaps imagine the atmosphere during the festivities. The other chambers cannot be explored alone.

1.55 We return the same way, climbing back up to the **ridge**. ***Alternative:*** the real mountain enthusiast will quickly ascend the 100 meters (altitude) up to the **summit of Mt. Papás** (419 m) in 20 min., take a quick look over to Santoríni, contentedly passing the chapel of Profitis Elias on the way to Panagía in one hour.

The more relaxed hikers will take the trails leading down
2.15 from the pass and, at the ditch, a monopáti to **Panagía.** Below the church we find "To Steki". Sometimes another kafeníon is open further on down.

Turn down left two houses below "To Steki" onto a mule
2.30 track. After the ditch at the end of the path there is a **field altar.** Proceed 30m uphill, over a wall and along a rather crumbling monopáti. Having passed around the walled vineyard on the right and climbed over another wall, you
2.40 meet the **way up** again, continue on down and turn left
3.15 at the fork towards **Ágios Geórgios.**

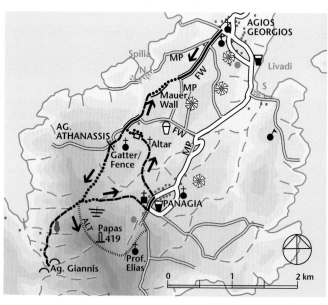

Koufonísia

The very small, flat island of Epano Koufonísia with sparse vegetation can become overcrowded in August (ferragosto). Most visitors are drawn by the long sandy beaches. There are few houses and no chapels outside the village as the island was only repopulated 200 years ago.

⑮ Round Tour of the Island

This practically level route of twelve kms along the west coast with its multicoloured rock formations leads to the wide sandy bay of Porí, then past several other sandy beaches back to the village. There is a tavern near the end of the trek.

AWT

0.00 From **St. George's Church** we take the road running through the village and head west, turning right at each of the two forks, going down to the bay with the island's shipyard (fig.). Captain Nikolas' fish taverna and an ouzerie fill up here in the evenings. We soon reach the protected fishing port along the dirt road. Behind it looms Naxos, huge in comparison with our tiny island.

0.15 ***Alternative:*** after the **wall** in the middle of the harbour boundary, we turn right into a field, cross it and come to a path further on, taking the left fork uphill. At the stone house above, we continue without a path, past shady picnic spots, on to the only hill of the island and, down from here, into the hollow (30 min.). See AWT 1.00 for continuation.

0.15 On the northern **side of the harbour,** a roadway leads along the brightly coloured rocky coastline, then we continue without a path until, 30 min. outside the harbour, the way climbs up a dry bed, where we come across a refuse

1.00 dump. We take the access road leading to a **hollow.** Here a footpath branches off left (red dots), at the end of which we climb over a wall, continuing first to the right of a field and then across country to reach the long sandy beach of

1.25 **Porí.** This is a good place to while – provided you have brought along something to drink.

> *Short cut:* a monopáti leads directly from the end of the beach onto a roadway to the village in 35 min.

There is a wide trail leading along the coast, past beautiful

1.55 sandy beaches, to the hotel complex of **Finikas.** Here you can fortify yourself at the shady beach taverna for the last

2.15 stage to **Chóra.**

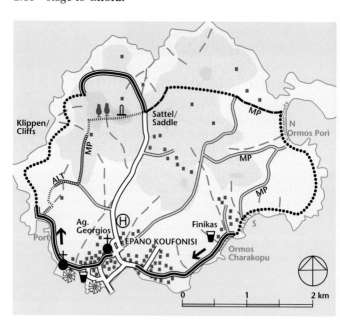

Mílos

The flat mining island is of volcanic origin and was built up gradually in layers by several volcanoes; however, the huge bay is not a caldera, but was formed by displacement. This large natural harbour was the cause of many invasions in the past. The natural beauties of this rather barren island face the sea: here one can walk and swim along the truly magnificent rocky coastline, surely one of the most beautiful of the Cyclades.

⑯ The Coast of Mílos

This four to five-hour hike leads along the north coast. There are no paths, but they are not necessary. You can walk in shorts and sandals with good soles. There are no tavernas on the beaches, some of which are deserted. The second part of the trek leads through wonderful rock formations. It is possible to cut short the tour half way.

Take the Pollonia bus to Fylakopí.

Fylakopí was the first capital of the island and the centre of the obsidian trade with the whole of the Mediterranean. Excavations have unearthed four towns built on top of each other, dating from between 2300 and 1100 BC. The frescoes discovered have now been moved to the National Museum. The untrained eye can still see a huge defence wall of cyclopean stonework and the layout of the interlocked houses on the site today.

AWT 0.00   The trek begins at the **bus station.** If you intend to end your hike in Mytakas, the return times of the buses are listed here. It is easy to find the rocky path between the road and the sea, which leads you to the first private bay between the rocks after three minutes. Having gone over a rocky tunnel **1**, then directly above the water, you arrive

0.10   in the holiday resort of **Papafraga.** Take the roadway here up right towards the sea and then bear left to the sandy bay. A roadway behind it leads up onto a sort of heath **2**, and from here you head back towards the rocky coast. Sea gulls from the island of Glaronissia opposite, do low-flying exercises here in the spring. At the end of the rugged, scree

0.25   landscape is the **small barrel-roofed church** of Ag. Konstantinos. Not until you get closer, can you see the hidden, small fishermen's houses and the harbour **3**. The rock in the sea ahead forms a double-spanned bridge **4**. After the church wall we turn off right, then immediately left, walking over solidified lava above a huge cave, which is not recognisable as such until later **5**. After the large sandy bay follows another smaller bay on the right. Now it is possible to walk right out along the spit before carrying on over the flat rock directly at the water's edge. Having broken away and now separated by a five-metre stretch of

water from the mainland, a large rock is occupied by raucous seagulls in the spring. We jump over long, narrow crevices in which the water bubbles. This unreal landscape **6** arose by the rock being compacted under repeated pressure. The remaining vegetation has been forced to the ground by the wind. There are rock pools, large enough to take a refreshing bathe in. The natural harbour of **Mytakas** with its small, picturesque houses, lies at the bend in the coastline.

0.50

> *Short cut:* you can walk on the road above in five minutes and stop the bus. Though the most beautiful rocks have still to come!

After we have passed the harbour, we reach a wide sandy bay with two tamarisks and two hewn caves. The wondrous world of the **Sarakiniko Coast** starts above. It consists of sandstone and limestone, eroded into rounded hollows by wind and water and polished into bizarre shapes. It is undoubtedly one of the most beautiful coastlines in Europe **7**. Flat rocks lie in the water, the steep cliffs above the sea sometimes taking on the appearance of a herd of elephants at a watering place. Wandering above the cliffs, you feel as if you were among desert dunes. Then a **dirt track**, down which rental cars and moped roar, leads down to the water **8**.

★

1.25

> *Alternative:* the sporty among us can wander on over the green crest of the next headland, arriving in the picturesque fishing village of **Mantrakia** in 15 minutes. The multicoloured rocks here are relics of the complicated geological formation of the island. From here, however, you have to go up another 25 minutes to Pero Triovassalos, not necessarily worth seeing, before reaching the bus station.

Pleasure-seekers stay on at the Sarakiniko Coast for a while, enjoying the rounded rock formations. Drinks can be bought in the cleft in the summer. When our eye is sated, we put our shoes back on, take about twelve minutes to go up the dirt track to the asphalt road, then go right along it for 70 m before heading over the ridge without a trail. The huge bay of Mílos is visible below and we find paths and tracks over some pretty unsightly terrain down to **Adámas**.

2.00

A short trek for pleasure-seekers:
Anyone just wanting to see the Sarakiniko Coast and who needs a lot of time for swimming and sunbathing, should take the bus only as far as the **Mytakas fork**, walk five minutes down to the harbour (AWT 0.50 of the main trek) and stroll on left from there.

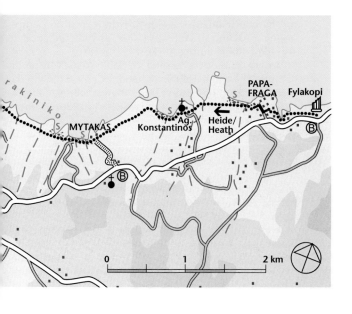

Mílos' History

*A four-hour trek from Adamas to the
most important historic sites and places of
cultural interest on the island. It is
advisable to wear long trousers – not just
because of the sacred places, but also
to protect your legs! Large stretches lead
without a path above the sea, offering
a magnificent view of the bay. It is possible
to stop for a break at a tavern in Klima
after an hour. Finding your way is easy,
but a degree of sure-footedness is required.
(See catacomb opening times below).*

AWT 0.00 Near the **harbour** in **Adamas**, in a cave on the right, are some hot springs. These hot public baths, which were found all over the island in earlier days, owe their existence to a the volcanic origins of Mílos. We follow the path north along the beach to the fishing bay and head on over the hill to the next, more peaceful bay. Here we come across a graveyard and a monument from 1897. It was set up in memory of the Frenchmen who died of the plague here in the harbour, aboard the ships of the expedition corps, during the Crimean War (1853 – 56). French soldiers were also buried here during the First World War.

Mílos was one of the earliest Cycladic islands to be inhabited. The vast natural harbour, one of the largest in the Mediterranean, has always been of great strategic importance and was the cause of the repeated conquests of the island through the ages.

Behind the monument, the path soon ends and we head

0.17 uphill to the **beacon** without a trail. Behind the beacon are traces of the island's most recent history. The builders were from Germany, as can be read on the torn concrete of the coastal fortification from 1943 ■. They had no reinforcing steel and used large rocks to join the concrete instead.

Above to the left, you see a rocky hilltop with a white marker post. Heading in this northerly direction up on the diagonal, you arrive on the next plateau at a huge, Stone Age weapons manufacture. Here below the fence, black obsidian, a compact vitreous rock which forms a crust on

streams of lava, was split and made into tools and weapons some 9000 years ago. We continue over the black rocks as if walking on coals **2**.

There is another monument on top of the last plateau – though we are too early to see anything: inside a fence, under the earth, are the remains of a settlement, still await-

0.30 ing the archaeologist's spade. We continue past the **fence** on our right and the marker post on our left, heading inland. Having rounded the mountain, we see Trypiti and Plaka **3**, crowned by the fortress of the Venetians, who ruled the island from 1207 to 1566, ahead. Passing the elongated rock on our left, we head further inland along the edge of the fields and come across a shed on a dirt track

0.45 leading left to Trypiti. Soon we reach a **rural chapel**, stood protectively in front of the olive tree next to it **4**.

> *Alternative:* half of the following way is pathless and leads through scrub. You can avoid it by walking straight towards Trypiti and descending to Klima.

A dirt road walled on both sides bears left directly after the chapel with the crooked olive tree. It leads around a farm-house, then runs on between vegetable fields above the

0.55 sea, leading to picture-book **terraces of olive trees 5**. Opposite, on the other side of the huge bay, the mountain of the Prophet rises up ahead – and, below, the ferries bring in holidaymakers, the new conquerors of the island.

Having torn your eyes from the beautiful view, you climb down five metres and follow the terrace along which a mule track leads further north. Where the terraces end, you have to climb over low walls and should keep uphill rather than down. There are terraces here too, though they are now covered in scrub. Soon you sight the fishing village of **Klima** below. It's advisable to keep right on the mountain when going down through the phrýgana as there are steep cliffs below! The way becomes rather steep directly above Klima. Left of the hotel "Panorama" (drinks only during the day), you climb down a narrow path to the pic-

1.15 turesque **harbour 6**. Here there are shady benches waiting beneath the tamarisks.

Proceed 300 m along the asphalt road into the gorge until you see the remains of the immense wall of the Dorian town of Melos, the historic highlight of the trek, up on the left. In order to get there, we climb up the white-painted steps which lead up left from the road, past a church in a cave. At the end of the steps, we walk a few metres along a worn, level path and then over pumice stone scree up to 1.25 the **catacomb** ticket office.

> *This underground cemetery, secretly laid out by the Christian community in the 3rd century AD, is the largest in Greece. 7000 to 8000 dead lie buried here. The first 30 m of the system of chambers are open to visitors. In the low season, they are closed on Mondays and close fairly early the rest of the week. Possibly, you should set off a little earlier!*

We continue along the newly laid path and arrive at the car park before heading on 80 m left along the road and turning left at the bend onto the sign-posted dirt track. To the right are parts of the Dorian town fortifications and, shortly afterwards, we come past the site where the "Venus" was found in 1820. We are now on the ancient 1.35 site of the classical city of **Melos**.

> *It was inhabited from 1000 BC to 1000 AD, having been founded by the Dorians who had previously destroyed Fylakopi. The Romans also later erected buildings on the*

site, including a well-preserved theatre **7**. *What an experience it must have been to sit in an elegant tunic and watch a play being performed against this grandiose natural backdrop!*

We go back along the same field track to the concrete road and, straight after the right bend, up the concrete ramp to the left. A relict from Byzantine times: a short monopáti, overlooked by the bulldozers. We cross the road and wander through the faceless, newly developed area of **Trypiti.** Only the thought that our times have produced some better buildings can help us here. The bus leaves from

1.45 near the **church**, below which there are two or three taverns with a peaceful evening view over to the sea **8**. Time, at last, to think of the colleagues back home.

Mykonos

The rather flat and infertile island is largely composed of granite. Wonderful beaches and the beautiful main town made it a holiday destination long ago. The widespread uncontrolled development of holiday homes on the island has brought with it a corresponding degree of road construction. As a result, very little remains of the old system of mule tracks. This book uses some of the remaining monopátia along which one can discover Mykonos on foot and take a closer look at the chapels (reportedly 365!), the dovecote towers and small farms and discover new beaches!

⑱ Traversing Mykonos I

In three and a half or four and a half hours across the centre of the island to Mykonos town, past a large convent and numerous small chapels, wide and secluded beaches.

AWT 0.00
We request the driver of the bus to Áno Méra to halt at the **bus stop** in **Paleokastro**. We follow the sign to Paleokastro ("old fortress") opposite and turn left at the fork. Five minutes later, we are in front of the convent **1** below a flat hill.

> *To strangers, the **Convent of Paleokastro** looks rather uninviting from the outside. Unexpected visitors used to be threatened with hot oil being poured onto them from above the entrance. Though today the doors are wide open. The ensemble dating from 1782 forms a rectangle consisting of living quarters joined by walls. In the very picturesque courtyard is a charming small church with a beautiful iconostasis and Jesus as mighty ruler/pantocrator in the cupola. (God the Father is represented by angels in the Orthodox Church).*

One is reluctant to leave the quiet, shady monastery courtyard. Outside we turn left along the severe facade, continuing past dilapidated dovecote towers up the hill. A lonely chapel stands on the large site of an earlier fort which controlled the centre of the island in Venetian times and was already fortified in antiquity. Nothing is left apart from pieces of crumbled wall and the remains of a cistern, but the wide view to both sides of the island are worth the climb. The view westwards **2** is of particular interest for us – our route leading beyond the reservoir.

0.12
Back down on the main **track again**, we turn left to the bay **3**.

> *Short cut:* opposite the chapel on the pass is a monopáti, a real rarity on Mykonos. If you go down this way, you will save an hour but miss out on a peaceful bay and a swim. (see map: ABK)

With the chapel on our right, we continue straight ahead past three more chapels and come to a cleft with a

0.35
concrete bridge and a chapel above it **4**. 50 m *before* the bridge, we climb down carefully over rough, natural ter-

0.50   races. A small, deserted **sandy bay** 5 – ideal for a refreshing swim – awaits us below.

After our dip, the way continues over cliffs, which drop
1.05   down deeply to the sea 6, and then to the **sandy bay of Ftelia.** Depending on the wind direction, there is sometimes a large amount of plastic debris washed up here. Excavations have been carried out at the elevation in the middle of the beach.

At the end of the bay is a restaurant where the way climbs uphill (chapel right). We now stroll towards the mountain ridge on the horizon: left through the gate at the fork and, below a house with a chapel 7, through another gate. Then on without a trail below the hill to the island's walled
1.30   **water reservoir,** bearing right here. Above the dam to the north, we soon come to the road to Agios Sortis.

> *Alternative:* along *right* it is a ten minute walk to the very beautiful and clean **sand dune beach of Panormos** with a tavern!

We walk 100 m left along the road and then right, up the concrete track. Later on, the way leads down and we keep a little over to the left without a trail until we cross a monopáti, which we follow to the chapel in the valley
2.00   before reaching the "**Bridge** of August 20" via the dry bed leading uphill to the right.

From here we march left and then straight on up the road until a footpath heads up right from a downhill left bend. The villa on the hill remains to the right above our path. This then leads down to a chapel where we turn right up the road and then immediately left again. Below the road we turn off left again at some houses onto a monopáti and thus avoid at least one stretch of the road. The view widens from the pass which follows, from Delos to Tínos; the road also widens 100 m further on. We go right downhill (not following the signs) and then left again straightaway. The modern docks are visible below, which doesn't exactly make the arrival any more romantic. We cross to the other side of the bypass and, 30 m ahead on the left, find the old foot-path leading down to Mykonos 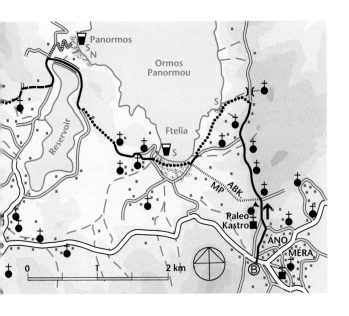. We should take our time here – the walls offering places to daydream! **Mykonos** will stay open the whole night.

★
2.40

Trip to Delos
As the ship returns at 3 p.m., there is not enough time for a proper trek. Moreover, large parts of the island are off-limits for tourists.

One possibility is an archaeological tour followed by a classical picnic on Mt. Kytharos. The selection of dishes and beverages should be commensurate with the dignity of the place of course!

⑲ Traversing Mykonos II

*A four-hour trek from Áno Méra
through a wide valley to the beaches in
the north-east.*

The well-fortified facade of the most powerful monastery on Mykonos **1** stands in the somewhat oversized main square of **Áno Méra**.

> *If you enter the **Monastery of Panagia Tourlani** through the narrow doorway, you will be surprised to see a highly ornate marble facade opposite. The monastery church with its campanile takes up a central position within the complex and is surrounded by hallways and monks' cells. A rarity is displayed in the church: the iconostasis created in 1775 by Florentine master craftsmen in an almost South American, rich, late baroque style. (Description in the forecourt).*

AWT 0.00 When you leave the **monastery**, turn right downhill and cross the road at the bus shelter. Below, before the dovecote **2**, head up left and then right, down along the asphalt road from the top. Many of the roads are now tarred on Mykonos: we are left with going along this road for 15 minutes, though there is barely any traffic.

Beyond, a little to the right, we see the mountain of Profitis Elias along with a few buildings and masts. We will later have to climb down to the sea from the saddle in front of it to the right!

0.09 So, on we head down the road and left at the **fork** onto the plain.

> ***Alternative***: a way leads up left at the next fork to the convent of Paleokastro.

We make fast progress along the road. Behind us, the two monasteries control the valley with its numerous, small rural churches **3**. We head straight on along the main road

0.15 until we come to a **chapel with a house 4**. Down right from here, past another chapel (left) and a house, whose owner would obviously preferred to have become a captain on a large sailing ship. To our right are some shady reeds. After the bridge, we go down left through the dry bed. (If it is wet, carry on along the concrete road, turning left at the end onto a footpath.)

50 m before the dry bed meets the road, we turn off right

onto a monopáti bordered by some reeds on the right (5,
from the opposite direction). On between two hills, we
come to a cistern, head up left here and proceed above the
fields through the attractive landscape. Having then
passed through a group of houses, we take the concrete

0.35 road left towards Mt. Elias. We reach the **main road** after
house no. 480.

> ***Short cut:*** going right will take you directly to the
> beach of Kalafatis.

Turn *left* onto the road then, 130
m further on, right opposite a
house onto a track across the
fields which soon curves to the
left. Between two houses **6**, a
monopáti heads straight on
towards Mt. Elias. When another
monopáti intersects, we either go
right or straight on, without a
trail, towards the asphalt road.

0.50 Bear up right at the **turning** and,
as soon as you see the sea, right
onto a path which forks again –
we first head down left and then,
without a trail, along the valley

1.15 floor to the **bay of Lia** **7** with a
taverna, some bungalows and a
sandy beach, along one half of
which are sunshades. If you prefer something quieter, go right,
across the rocks to reach a private,

rocky cove after three minutes, or on even further, through bizarre rocks, to a tiny sandy beach.

Again we must surmount rocks and walls until we reach the shade of the tamarisks on the 600 m long beach of
1.45 **Kalafatis.** The bus stop is in front of the hotel. If you don't overly like the tavernas and sunshades here, you can trek on further to the picturesque fishing village of **Dimasto** 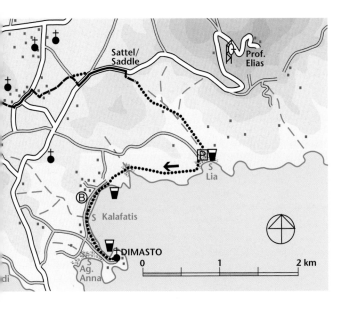 on a peninsula. Apart from the beach of Ag. Anna, there is also a very pleasant taverna here.

For the avid trekker: why not combine ⑱ and ⑲! After eight to nine hours, you'll know how big Mykonos is.

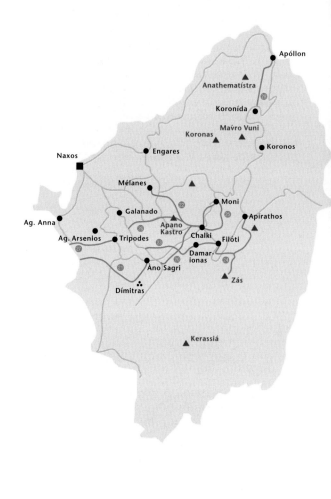

Naxos

Naxos is the vibrant centre of the Cyclades. Young and old, Greek and Greenlander alike stroll along the harbour. It is popular among walkers due to its varied landscape. One encounters high mountain ranges of granite and gneiss with marble, broad, fertile plains with plentiful water supplies and long, sandy beaches. It can even rain in the mountains during the summer!

In the main hiking area of the Tragéa plateau, an ideal Greek landscape, one wanders through extensive olive groves and small oak forests, past ancient Byzantine churches. The hiking trails are sometimes overgrown and difficult to identify due to the dense vegetation. A good German map of the island 1 : 50 000 is available from the tourist information at the harbour, the bus timetable from the adjacent bus station.

Taxis can be ordered anywhere under the number 24331. The tourist information can also provide well-versed guides.

⑳ Into the Plain of Tragéa

An easy trek to whet your appetite, through the olive groves of the Tragéa plain. Two and a half hours over easily identifiable tracks and paths with a pleasant stop at a taverna in Chalki.

The most difficult part comes straightaway: explaining to the conductor that you want to get off at the turning to Agiassos (or Timios Stavros). Here you head along the road **AWT 0.00** between the **petrol station** and the windmills, up to the bulky, unadorned **pýrgos of Timios Stavros** ■.

> *The original 17th century fortress-tower of the Baséou family was later converted into a monastery. A fertile plain, which reaches right down to the sea, spreads out below – watched over by the Temple of Demeter on the hill in the centre.*

Directly behind the monastery, a path ascends up over slabs of rock into the olive groves. You wander along cheerfully: to our left, the wide valley protected by the Venetian castle up on the highest mountain. Then turn right at the

0.10 fork to the **reservoir.** The dirt track leading past the olive groves is lined with nut bushes ■ ■. In September, preparations are made for the harvest: tightly woven nets are spread beneath ■ the olive trees and the olives then knocked off. At the next fork, wander straight on to the hollow where you come across an attractive paved stone path through a field. Bear right ahead of the fence, down onto a shady path which later becomes a wide dirt track. Soon the beautiful plain of Tragéa, which remains green all year, lies ahead. The torso of a windmill is visible up left on a hill; but we march on unwaveringly below. The dirt track makes a left-hand bend – at this very spot begins our

0.30 footpath up to the **small church** on the hilltop ■. If you prefer not to take a break here, continue downhill along the track, taking in the attractive, green surroundings as you go. On the right, between some trees, you have a view of the hamlet of Damalas and, above in the distance, you see the mountain village of Moni. When you come to the vehicle bridge alongside a chapel, turn right and, 50 m further on, bear left onto a roadway lined by ancient olive trees. Later, at the junction, we naturally take the

more attractive way down right into a dry bed, before
0.50 going up a few steps to **Himarros** and the road. Here, the
relentless Cycladic wanderers among us head uphill past
the cemetery, turning right at the small church on top
before heading down again, contentedly, over a splendid
paved path and on left below.

> *Short cut:* the others go right along the asphalt road
> and, 400 m further on, turn off left between a house
> and a chapel **7**.

You take the unsurfaced way straight ahead and turn
down right into the dry bed (blue arrows) immediately
after. On the other side is a sunken way leading into the
village.

> ▶ by heading through the olive groves left of the
> path, you can reach the beautiful, though locked,
> church of **Ágios Geórgios o Diassoritis** (George the
> Rescuer), an attractive example of a Byzantine cruci-
> form domed basilica of the Tragéa. The way is sign-
> posted in Chalki.

1.10 Keeping right at the first houses in **Chalki**, we take a look
onto the square to see who else is sitting in front of Yiannis'
taverna.

Later on, you can wait for the bus at the church of Proto-
thronos **8**.

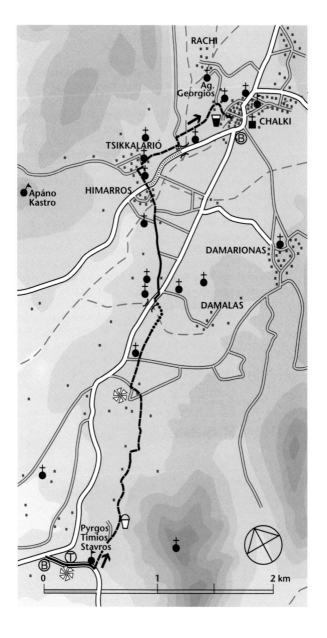

RACHI

Ag.
Georgios

CHALKI

B

TSIKKALARIÓ

Apáno
Kastro

HIMARROS

DAMARIONAS

DAMALAS

Pyrgos
Timios
Stavros

B   T

0   1   2 km

㉑ The Temple of Demeter

A four-hour trek to the partially re-erected Temple of Demeter and on over a plateau with tilled fields to the long, sandy beach of Plaka. There are no tavernas en route; long trousers are an advantage.

AWT 0.00 We jump off the bus at the **Sagrí turning** and march 600 m along the road to the village of **Ano Sagrí**. (Sometimes the bus stops nearer the houses). Turning right ahead of the village, we bear left of the monument in the small grove of pines, down onto the concrete road and then left later on along the paved path, to the deserted monastery

0.10 of **Agios Eleftérios ❶**. (Though it is certainly worthwhile going on few steps to see the small, clustered village!)

Opposite the monastery, to the right of a stone gentleman with a bow tie, we climb down the steps and wander along a defile in the direction of a chapel on the hill, which lies above us on the right. We go a short stretch along a worn path and then onto the dirt track below the hill chapel. Do not follow the sign to the Temple of Nikolaos, but head straight on along the dirt track ❷. On the left, you see a wide plain with olive trees and, opposite at an angle, the temple ❸ on a hill. Our dirt track ends above a shed, and we follow a red arrow to the right, before climbing down left (arrow) into a hollow. At first we go right without a trail for a short stretch, and then left at the monopáti, to the middle of the valley through the dry bed. We arrive at

0.30 the **temple** along hidden paths.

*The **Temple of Demeter** (possibly also dedicated to Apollon) dates from the 6th century BC. It was used for diverse purposes and rebuilt several times during the course of history. It was nevertheless possible to ascertain its original form and reconstruct some (40 %) of it to date.*

You now return along the original path and, directly behind the temple, join onto a roadway into the valley, past the small museum. Continue without a trail under some olive trees through a hollow, then uphill through the phrýgana until you come across the monopáti you used earlier. Turn left here. On our left above is the re-erected temple: we can take pleasure in the fact that an ancient temple has again become part of this delightful landscape

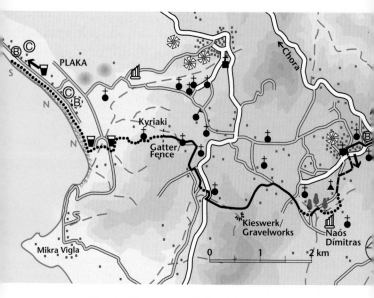

which holds a close relationship with the mountains and the wide plain. A site which only the ancient Greeks could have chosen!

0.40   We next trudge on through a **hollow**, which is sometimes wet, take a dirt track on the right immediately after and then, before the olive grove, make our way up left without a trail to the saddle. Heading along the road at the top in a northerly direction, we take a look back towards the temple! Our point of departure in Ano Sagrí is visible up

0.50   on the right. At the **crossing** (sign in the opposite direction: Dímitras) the way leads straight on **4**. We are surrounded by wide fields and solitary, shady trees, much punished by the wind: ideal resting spots for both humans and animals.

1.00   Now take the left fork at the **junction** leading over the hill which marks the boundary of the plain. The dirt road **5** passes a gravel works (left) on the way down and ends at

1.20   the **road**. We have to march energetically 100 m along it to the right, until we are below the chapel **6** on the slope. Opposite (on the left-hand side of the road) is a walled entrance leading down to some fields. Head across country for 120 m until you find a dirt road leading up right from the hollow. Later on, when some walls appear up ahead, turn left along the path and then, shortly after, bear right ahead of the farmhouses.

We enjoy the peaceful dirt road  between the rocks which
1.45 leads us to the **slope** above the sea, where there is a break between the rocks. At first we head down along a track-like path, then without a trail over thorny terrain to the Kyriakí chapel at the foot of the slope **8**. Then on from the
2.00 **chapel**, along farm roads lined with reeds, to the wide
2.10 **dunes** ahead, where we tear off our clothes!

To reach the bus into the town, it takes another 35–40 minutes via the beach, where we have the opportunity to examine both the architecture of the sand-castles and
2.50 the stature of their creators. The **bus** leaves from the camp-site. Length approx. 11 km.

Language problems?

Let the pictures do the talking
1200 objects at your fingertips

Picture
dictionary
64 pages
9 × 13 cm

$ 5,95
£ 3,99
€ 4,99

point it®

Traveller's
language
kit

Picture
dictionary

ISBN
3-9803130-2-6

Graf Editions

㉒ Koúros, the Youth

*A three to four-hour trek to the colossal
statue of the koúros of Phlerio and then on
to Melanés. For the most part without
defined paths, but the way is easy to find.
Please note that there are just four and
a half hours between the arrival of the first
bus in Chalki and the return journey
from Koúros. It is necessary to enquire as
to the bus times. At a push, you may
have to call a taxi (Tel. 2 43 31).*

AWT 0.00 You take the first bus to **Chalki,** turn down the **lane** to the
right of the kafeníon and go past the square and the at-
tractive taverna. Unfortunately, we don't have time today!
Head right on the road below, out of the village, and 300 m

0.06 along the road, between olive groves, up to a **bridge** with
a small building **❶**. Turn right here along an attractive
stony path and then left straight after, up an idyllic way to
the village of **Tsikkalarió.** On the edge of the village, there
is a small church overlooking the plain of Tragéa. It strikes
us that many of the houses in this delightful landscape
have tiled roofs, the reason being that it rains quite often.
The way through the houses is fairly flat. From the **end of**

0.18 **the village** you can see the ruins of the mountain fortress
of Apáno Kastro **❷** in the middle of a moonscape, and
come to a wall in a green valley above.

> *Alternative: if you climb up left in front of the wall, you
> reach a plateau of rock. A **burial site** from Geometric
> times (750 BC) has been excavated here. A rock stood on
> end, similar to a menhir, is visible; and above it, Apáno
> Kastro **❷**. You can just make out some 30 circular or
> elliptical tombs, measuring up to twelve metres in dia-
> meter. The burial gifts found in the dolmen, including
> ceramics, gold jewellery and charred figs and nuts, are on
> view in a raised cabinet at the Museum of Archaeology in
> Chóra.*

0.30 To the *right* of the wall, a path leads up to the **chapel** on
the pass. From here you go on 200 m up to a small, hidden
doorway in the wall on the left.

> *Those wanting to storm the fortress must climb up ten
> minutes from here. The old Venetian Castel d'Alto, now*

Apáno Kastro, lies in ruins and looks across to Naxos town and the island of Paros.

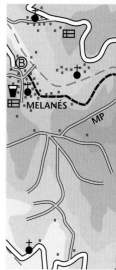

From below the fortress, we descend without a path through the rocks to the Phlerio plateau, which has something mystical about it. Above a large rock, is a door in the fence, and to the left, a place you can climb over it. Three rocks **3** are stood on the edge of the valley, which is green in the spring. It's easy to find your way along left of the oleander-lined creek and on the slope **4**. The Castel guards the valley from the rear. At the end of the valley, we pass a walled field with wind-bent trees on our right. Across the

1.00 **stream bed** and then later directly in the bed itself **5**, the going is slow between the oleander bushes. A fence has to be surmounted in the dry bed. It's best to stay in the stream bed until it becomes a

1.15 **concrete track.** After a few hundred metres over concrete, though beneath huge trees **6** and a wall of reeds on one side, there are several signs pointing left. From the other

1.20 direction they read: **Koúros**, the youth in the garden!

*Koúros statues represent gods or heroes. This prostrate statue **7** dates from around the 6th century BC and was probably intended for the Holy Grove on Delos. It was never completed due to a flaw in the material and remained in this position in the ancient quarry.*

This koúros belongs to the Kondili family, who also owns the well-tended garden around it. You can order snacks and drinks.

Having fortified yourself, you head left from Koúros along the concrete track you came on, going up to the bus stop at the crossing. However, there is no bus in the late afternoon!

If you want to thumb a lift, walk 600 m up right to the main road.

If you prefer to order a taxi to Melanés, head straight on over the crossing, along the concrete track which later

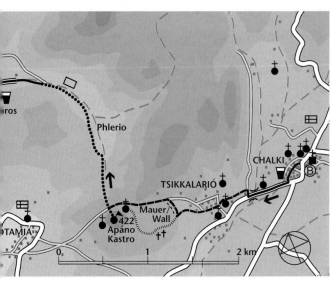

1.25 becomes a dirt track. The **fork** to the left with the sign "Melanés" is the wrong way; we go *straight on* (towards the dead-end), around the hill, until Melanés comes into view on the slope above a terraced valley **8** a short time later. You arrive in the lower part of the rather austere village of

1.40 **Melanés.** There is an interesting view above the slope opposite: the summit has been carved up by human hand and borne away: marble from Kinidaros.

Otherwise, there is nothing to write home about.

㉓ Venetian Pýrgi

A four-hour trek, at first along the old main road through the island, protected by ancient tower-houses or pýrgi, and on through Arcadian landscapes to Filóti. These medieval fortress-towers were the easily defensible country residences of the Venetian nobility. Around 30 such towers still exist on Naxos.

AWT 0.00

It's best to tell the bus driver where you want to get off shortly before you get there, i.e. **Káto Sagri.** (There is a marble factory on the left, just before the road turns off to K.S.). The bus stops at a stone **bus shelter** opposite the road to Káto Sagri. You follow the tail of the disappearing bus for 200 m along the road, leaving it at a right bend and turning onto a dirt road **1** straight ahead. There is a power line and, usually, a cow on the left. On the way down, you see the first inhabited pyrgos **2** against the backdrop of Apáno Kastro, the main Venetian fortress in the hinterland of the island (㉒, ㉖). In the valley below, lies a large, noble country residence of a newer kind. We cross the

0.13

dry bed, taking the roadway up left to the church on the hill shortly after. Go straight on ahead at the fork and turn off right at the left bend onto the wide, old road paved with flat rocks **3**, which used to lead from the Tragéa plateau to the harbour. From the paved road we can soon see a beautiful, old (but regretfully locked) cruciform-domed basilica **4** and another pyrgos (Baséou or Tímios Stavrós, ㉑) in the background. Then, after some ruins on the right-hand side, the track becomes lost in the rock and we let ourselves be guided by the wall on the left.

★

0.30

Having past a polygonal building, you come to the **road**, which you cross in the direction of a windmill torso. (There is a rather tall pasture fence ahead of the windmill, however, which you can avoid by going left along the road for a short stretch). Behind the windmill, you head down to a roadway, which you follow to the right for ten metres before turning off left again straight after.

We are now on the fertile Tragéa plain with its large olive groves. High walls on our right **5** lead us safely through,

0.50

past the small village of **Damalás** in the hollow, protected

by an attractive domed church 6. We hike on to the village
1.00 of **Damarionas.** Right at the start of the village, at the
corner of a house 7, we head into a maze of alleyways,
1.05 turning right before an archway and then down to the **war
memorial** on the asphalt road.

> *Alternative:* you can reach
> Chalki over attractive mule
> tracks in 15 minutes: take
> the steps to the left of the
> memorial, keep left at the
> fork, go right behind the
> bridge and then on left again
> straight after, passing the
> sports field on your right,
> go through the hollow and
> then, keeping left, you'll
> arrive at the washing facili-
> ties in Chalki.

Our way to Filóti leads up right
from the monument. At the fork
with the panoramic café-table
view, you bear left and are soon at
the upper end of the Tragéa plain
on a roadway with a great view,
surrounded by olive trees. No
matter how hard you try, you will
not lose your way here and, thus
have all the time in the world to

look out for more pýrgi. Three can be seen at once – two in Chalki and one in Keramío.

Below Filóti we take the bridge over the hollow, then the dirt road right straight after and wander on up, between gardens with a view over to Mt. Zás, to the inviting street
1.30   cafés of **Filóti**. The clever patron of course knows exactly when the next bus will arrive and that there is time to stop and have something under the plane trees before. If you're interested, you'll also find a pyrgos here in Filóti.

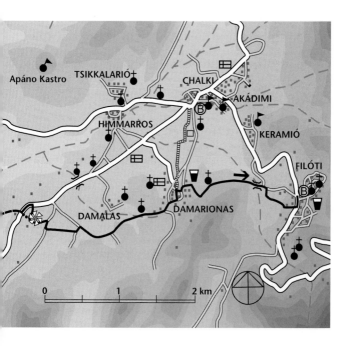

㉔ Zeus Almighty!

A physically demanding, six-and-a-half-hour trek of twelve kilometres between Filóti and Apírathos with an ascent of the highest Cycladic peak, Za, Zás, Zefs or Zeus at 1001 or 1004 m – in Greece there are always several alternatives, as indeed with this hike: with or without the summit, Filóti or Apírathos. Food for the journey, long trousers and perhaps a windcheater for higher up are recommendable.

You should be sat in the first bus to Filóti today!

Short cut: don't get off the bus until the turning (Greek: diakladosi) to Danakós, from where it takes eight minutes to Ag. Maria (AWT 0.30).

AWT 0.00 From Filóti **bus station** head 700 m along the road to the end of the village (or get off at the second bus stop in Filóti). Where the road begins to curve right, follow a
0.07 **monopáti** going left up the slope **1** along whose upward incline you soon come across a chapel. Keeping right later
0.20 on at the fork, continue on up to the **road.**

Alternative: on the route described below, some walls have to be surmounted (1.7 m) at the top. You can just as well remain on the road, taking the right fork above (Danakós) to St. Mary's Chapel **2**.

Otherwise you continue 50 m left along the road and then scramble up 50 m until you cross a beaten path; go up right along it, past some ruins. The path becomes a mule track and then forks – you go left, heading on uphill! In the vineyards on the pass are the walls mentioned above: now
0.30 climb over them, landing directly at **St. Mary's Chapel 2**.

Short cut: without ascending the peak, you cross the road in the direction of Fotodóti (see AWT 2.25).

Those aiming for the summit should go right from St. Mary's Chapel, along the defile. You soon reach a fence with a house on the left and, further on, a drinking trough on the right. When the path peters out ahead, arrows, cairns and other hikers serve as route markers instead. At times the way is covered with dense, thorny scrub **3**, but stops higher up. In Zeus' case, it is the same as with other elderly gentlemen: a fringe of hair below and a bald patch

1.30   on top. Heading on over the bald patch to the **summit of Zás**, you see an almost vertical drop beyond.

The Greeks seem to have great respect for this peak: there is neither a chapel nor a mast at the top to disturb the majesty of the greatest of the Greek gods. Though at the top we drink to Dionysos and his island, Naxos. But beware, our destination in Apírathos to the north is still quite some way!

2.25   Back down the same way! At **St. Mary's Chapel**, a decision as to the way to continue must be reached.

> *Short cut:* Back to Filóti. (See map: ABK).

If you intend to continue, cross the road and take the level track straight ahead to Fotodóti. We wander above terraces and gardens **4**, beneath oaks and olive trees with a spring in our step, until we see what looks like an enchantingly situated Venetian fortress-tower **5**. It is in fact a fortified

2.50   **monastery.**

> *The unlocked **Moni Fotodóti** with its attractive green forecourt is thought to have been founded by a Byzantine princess. Lord Byron was here before us, of course!*

Back on our previous track, we turn right and continue to the left of a vineyard along a quiet path to the opposite

3.00   slope and, keeping right, head up to the **pass**. There is a gate here, and another directly *opposite,* barely visible in a fence (red dots). Then we see Apírathos on the other side of the valley again.

★   It is wonderful strolling along the monopáti above a plateau **6** up to a second pass above the wide valley. Here you have to keep right while going downhill over the zigzags to the fork; then climb down *left* and through the ditch. Over a stony path, then without a path, you come

3.20   to a small **retaining weir** on the floor of the second valley, which is passable even in spring. You proceed along a wet path on the other side for a short way, then bear right over dry ground again, turning down right at the oak before going back up left to the next oak **7**. Then head up left

3.45   from some small reservoirs. In **Apírathos** you have to find your way through some confusing marble steps, but are soon sat either on the plátia, one of the most attractive on the Cyclades **8**, or tranquilly at "Lefteris" (below) under a walnut tree with a view of the valley. Zeus Almighty, that was a long way! And it's still another five minutes to the bus.

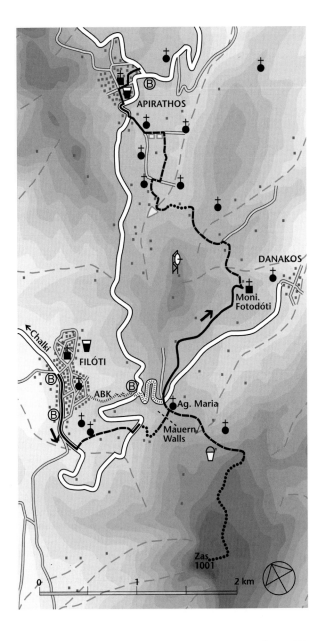

APIRATHOS

DANAKOS

Moni.
Fotodóti

←Chalki

FILÓTI

ABK

Ag. Maria

Mauern/
Walls

Zas
1001

0   1   2 km

㉕ Drosiani, Lady of the Morning Dew

An overwhelmingly beautiful trek of four to five hours. The route leads over wonderful monopátia, past the ancient church of Drosiani and through the Tragéa plateau, where orientation can be a little difficult. You can stop in tavernas in Moni or Chalki.

The bus needs half an hour to Halki, **Chalki** or Hal. It stops at the famous church Panagía Protothrónou: the key can be picked up from the papás. (Though no-one knows where he is at the moment.) So let's head down the **lane to the right of the kafeníon**, and then, the second on the right.

AWT 0.00

If you walk on 10 m, you'll run the risk of postponing your plans: the plátia is a picture-book Greek square with the taverna "Yiannis" and a hairdresser. Be resolute!

The second lane right (see above) leads us through gardens along the edge of the village. We cross a road and bear left at a fork ahead (sign Ag. Diassoritis). We continue straight on and, where necessary, left. On the right is a **church** built above a cistern. Turn left downhill here (sign as above) and go straight on until you see the hamlet of Rachi **1**. Next, cross the dry bed, turn right in **Rachi** ahead of the chapel, detouring it, and pass the double chapel **2** on your left at the other end of the village. Bear right here at the ruins.

0.05

0.08

★

You now head on over one of the most beautiful Cycladic trails of all **3**, keeping parallel to the opposite slope on the left. Our half-way destination, Moni, is visible above right in the hills. You turn down left at the fork to the grove of oaks and up right at the next (paved track). To your left, on the opposite slope, the ruins of a church with three naves has come into view, though its interior has little to offer. When you have **drawn level** with the church, climb up a steep, naturally stepped path on the right to the superb site of the locked church of **Damiótissa 4**.

0.20

Continue up over the hill, turning left at the bottom straight after, down a gentle incline through large olive groves into a dry bed and on, above the left side of the stream, where you are aided by red marker dots. Crossing to the other side further ahead, the stream is now on your left. Press on through the "stream", between oleander

bushes and man-high dragon arum , which lures insects with an odour of rotten meat. Further ahead, there are paths leading up both right and left. The defile on the *right* has been blocked off with branches, to stop the goats. *We* climb over them onto a shady defile which leads to a wide track over the fields. Here we head straight on. There are cisterns to the left, in a fenced-off vineyard. At the end of the fence we bear left, back to the stream, turning down steeply at the picturesque, but ruined, draw well into the dry bed, up the other side and then on to the right. Having sprung lightly over some walls, and passed through some

0.40 olive groves, you come to a locked **gate.** From the gate, you climb down to the stream, go across it and find a magnificent monopáti leading uphill on the other side. Briskly over the road at the top and onto another wonderful

0.45 **monopáti.** Bear left at the fork towards a campanile in an olive grove.

> **Panagia Drosiani,** *"Our Lady of the Morning Dew" is the oldest church on the island. The exterior has unfortunately been incorrectly restored. Inside are three smaller, cave-like aisles built at an angle onto the nave. The frescoes are famous: in the main cupola, the oldest layers are as much as 1400 years old and thus the most ancient in the Balkans. This church is open!*

0.50 Back at the fork, you stroll up to the outskirts of **Moni.** If you don't intend to go to a taverna, amble on up the slight incline through the village, which has little worth seeing. At the other end, you go right past a chapel , then turn off left, heading down a gentle slope which leads to the

0.55 **washing troughs** just beyond the village. A small path leads up from here to some terraced gardens. On the way

1.00 up, we come to a recently built **concrete bridge**, and bear *right* downhill before heading back up right after the dry bed. On the other side, we continue over even ground

1.10 level with the village along to a **dirt track**, and stride down it to the right. On the left we soon see a small, pretty

1.15 **monopáti** (with two small, red dots) which forks left. We do too! There are two windmill torsos on a hill to the right. Heading downhill between some rocks, the Tragéa plain and its villages, towered over by three Venetian fortress-towers and the dome of the church of Kaloxylos, soon lie ahead of us. Up here there are ***places to stop off with a view over to Mt. Zás.

There is no getting lost on the way down. The dome of Kaloxylos is our goal. Two rural chapels lie among the olive
1.35 trees on the left 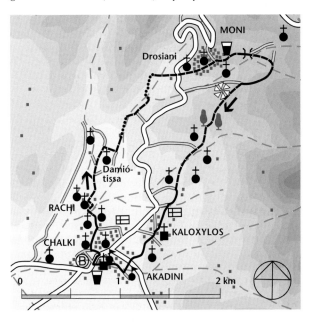. Below, on the other side of the **dry bed**, the way leads up over rock, then on through olive groves. Along the way there are a few houses and some washing facilities (left), a bridge and a graveyard. Soon we are stood in front of the Triáda church with its large dome. And no-one knows where the papás can be found (see above). From here we march right, down the hill to the road, and are
1.55 guided by the Venetian Gratsia tower back to **Chalki.**
If you are unlucky, you may end up at the Papadaki tower in Akadini, a neighbouring village. In which case it will take a few minutes longer. Perhaps there is still time for a glass at "Yiannis" (see above) anyway.

㉖ Apáno Kástro, the Venetian Fortress

A four to five-hour hike which leads up on a pleasant gradient through the well-watered, green valley of Potamiá. Anyone wanting to, can later climb up a steep slope to what used to be the main fortress of the Venetians. Water is available everywhere and there is an attractive garden taverna in Áno Potamiá. Please read where to get off the bus beforehand!

Tell the driver that you want to get off *after* Galanádo (gr.: *metaxy* Galanádo), above Ágio Mámas, (Thélo na katevó amésos metá ton Ágio Máma?). After Galanádo there is a petrol station on the left. Some 400 m on, the road leads over a pass (unfinished building on the right) from where you can see another valley and numerous peaks to the left. Here's our stop!

> *Gone too far? Stop off at the next large left bend in 1 km and take the somewhat overgrown alternative route.*

From the pass the next stage of the route is visible: the three parts of Potamiá can be seen in the green fold of the slope opposite and, on the steep cliffs to the right above, our intermediate destination – Apáno Kástro.

AWT 0.00   An inconspicuous path leads down from the **pass 1** into the valley (straight on at the fork) from where a barrel-roofed chapel and then the old church of Ágio. Mámas **2** soon come into view on the right. Take a few steps to the

0.12   right along the path running across below. As the **portal** has long been locked, you just climb over the wall and continue down to the empty barrel-roofed chapel. You turn right along the roadway below and, 50 m further on, note the place you have to turn down left later on.

> *After a few metres, you come to the ruins of the seat of the archbishop built in 1707 and those of the picturesque cruciform domed basilica of **Ágio Mámas.** Built in the 9th century, it was the main church on the island as well as the seat of the archbishop at the time; and, during Venetian rule, the seat of the Catholic archbishop.*

We hike back again over the overgrown vehicle tracks down right. The next leg of the journey, the monopáti near the ruins, is visible on the other side of the valley **3**.

0.25 Turning up to the right from the **ditch**, you come across a splendid path (photo, back cover) leading through groves of olives. Cypresses shape the tableau of the intensively cultivated valley. We continue straight on at a fork,

0.40 through a hollow and up to **Káto Potamiá**. The church (a garden taverna without a kitchen below, a tap in the churchyard) remaining to our left, we bear right into an alley and carry straight ahead on a gentle incline through the village. Some 200 m out of the village, we come across a fork above a manhole cover, go left uphill and enjoy the

★ wonderful stretch through olive trees ◪ above two Venetian pýrgi. Just before the next village, below right in a dry bed, are the romantic ruins of a pyrgos. It is not locked, so we can see the vaulted ceilings of differing heights. There are embrasures on the top floor.

0.50 Soon we arrive in **Méssi Potamiá**. Having turned up left at the fork by the basin, we pass a well, proceeding uphill towards a chapel ◪. From here we head right and then, at a chapel with a tiled barrel roof, down left before following a stream ◪. At the fork, from which a wide, stepped path leads up straight ahead, we *turn left* onto the main route

1.00 through the upper part of **Áno Potamiá**. We now need to keep our eyes open: in the alley on the left are steps to sit on and a disused well opposite ◪. (If you carry on here,

going downhill later, you come to the popular garden tavern "Pigi"). We go left past the well, up the steps of Odos Nikolaoy Orfanoy to the

1.05 **asphalt road.** Just opposite, a roadway runs straight on up in the direction of Apáno Kástro. At a left bend, the practised Cycladic eye spots a mule track leading up to the saddle, left of the fortress-topped mountain. 80 m on from a ruined chapel

1.20 is an **opening** through the wall from where we

1.30   climb right up a steep incline, without a trail, to **Apáno Kástro**. Phew!!

> *This was the main Venetian fortress, known at the time as Castel d'Alto, or upper fortress, in contrast to the lower fortress in Chóra. The rock had been inhabited since historical times, as is proven by ancient wall remains and burial sites, and was fortified by the Venetians a second time in the 13th century.*

On the opposite (southern) side we climb down to the horeshoe-shaped turret. Here was the entrance to the anterior fortress. We continue, heading left to the chapel on the pass where we go through an opening in the wall, this now being on our right. We next wander across some terraced fields with a wide view over to Mt. Zeus and the plateau of Tragéa **8** stretching before it. Further down, we

1.55   wander between huge rocks on to the village of **Tsikkalarió** where we stay on the main track before turning left at the wash area and car park below. Along a green, shady footpath, under oaks and mistletoe, we arrive down at a crossing at the road below. If you don't want to take the road to Chalkí, walk 40 paces up left and then down right

2.10   onto a path. This leads (through a dry bed) to **Chalkí.** Keeping to the right, we come to some tavernas where one can relax while waiting for the bus.

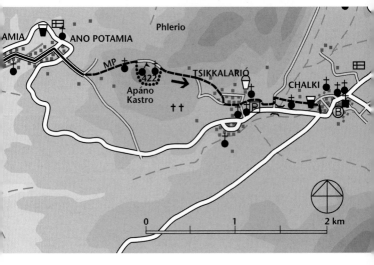

㉗ To the Dunes of Pláka

From Vívlos (Trípodes) we climb down an attractive, though somewhat overgrown path (long trousers recommended) onto a fertile plain and wander on between the fields to the sand dunes of Pláka.

AWT 0.00   In the **ditch** at the southern end of the village of **Vívlos**, below a large church with several towers, is a vehicle track which leads along the edge of the large valley to two chapels. You go right past the first chapel enclosed by a

0.15   fence. In front of the second, **St. George's Chapel**, you turn left below the ruins of a watchtower and then right 60 m further on, onto a path leading down to a rural chapel. Here you make your way to the right through some reeds, then a few metres uphill until you come across a secluded path where you bear right. You soon come to a

0.20   **grotto chapel** between the rocks. The next part of the trail down to the plain has now become somewhat overgrown.

0.35   Turning left along the dry bed in the **plain** below, you find paths lined with reeds. Near the ruins of the ancient tower on your right hand, you head right to the concrete path. Following this left, you proceed along the two rocky hills, arriving on dirt roads again. They do not lead straight to the sea, so it is perhaps better to take a shorter route across a field. Or you could follow the signs to Mikri Vigla, taking the right fork down to the hotel resort on the sea front. One way or another, you arrive at the endless sand dune

1.10   beach of **Pláka**. Sometimes the bus departs only from Maragas campsite.

㉘ Apollon or Dionysos?

After a dramatic bus journey of almost two hours through the mountains of Naxos, you wander over a gentle downhill incline to the huge, unfinished monumental statue near Apóllonas. The bus timetable allows 4 1/2 hours for the route! There are taverns both at the start and the end of the trek.

AWT

0.00 You take the first bus to **Koronida** (Komiakí) and then head towards the cemetery at the end of the village. Our route then forks off to the left, between a basketball field and the war memorial on the top of the mountain. The well marked trail offers wide sea views on its gradual descent, past a few ruins and

1.05 trees, down to the **road** which we follow uphill to right as far as the next right bend. At the "dead end" sign our way continues down left into a shady, green valley with a bridge, before climbing up again to the road leading down. The "Koúros" sign at the fork directs us left to the steps leading to the

1.40 **monumental statue** of over 10 metres. On account of its beard, it is assumed that the statue was intended to represent Dionysos. But it could also be a fragment of an Apollo figure which was not completed owing to faulty material. Since then the unfortunate god has been lying on an uncomfortable slant in the marble quarry for some 2,500 years to date. Obliquely opposite, on the other side of the road, is the

1.45 way down to **Apóllonas**.

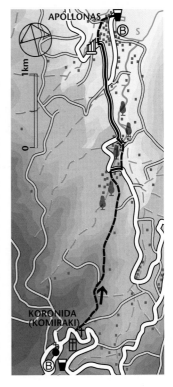

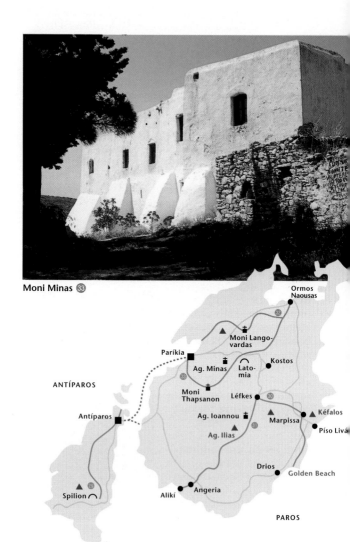

Moni Minas 33

Ormos
Naousas

Moni Lango-
vardas

Paríkia

Kostos

ANTÍPAROS

Ag. Minas

Lato-
mia

Moni
Thapsanon

Léfkes

Antíparos

Ag. Ioannou

Marpissa

Kéfalos

Ag. Ilias

Píso Livá

Drios

Golden Beach

Spilion

Aliki

Angeria

PAROS

Paros, Antiparos

In the centre of this ancient marble island lies
a secluded region of low-lying mountains with
wealthy monasteries, surrounded by fertile
farmland stretching down to the sea. The hiking
trails are accordingly varied. You are quite
alone on the gently sloping trails of the interior,
whereas towards the coast one occasionally
meets a farmer. The ancient Byzantine road
across the island is very popular among walkers
on the Cyclades.

Naoussa

㉙ The Cave of Antiparos

A walk of three and a half hours along dirt tracks leading through gently undulating landscape. Easy orientation, no kafenía en route, though a wonderful sandy beach to conclude with.

The first boat leaves for Antiparos from the well-known windmill at the harbour of Parikia at 9.30 a.m. (then hourly). As you need an hour to reach the cave and another half an hour to explore it, you should set off early. The enjoyable boat journey along the coast takes us past the island of Saliagos, on which the remains of a 7,000 year-old settlement were found, the oldest on the Cyclades.

It is only possible to buy a return ticket for the bus journey ahead. The driver demonstrates little sympathy when we tell him something about "hiking back". He will doubtless answer: "problems", as do all true Greeks.

> *Alternative:* sometimes it is possible to go by kaíki and hike up to the cave in half an hour.

AWT 0.00

After visiting the cavern **1**, which extends to a depth of 90 m, we climb up left outside onto the **roof of the cave** and walk in a north-easterly direction to the next hilltop. A path **2** with red markings runs next to it on the left, level with the hilltop. From the pass, the way leads down towards a semi-decayed house. Our destination, the chóra of Antiparos, is already visible in the background. A new dirt road leads to the house from the other side, having destroyed the old footpath.

The old path behind the ruin is still visible at first, but then disappears underneath the new dirt road **3**. We follow it around the next bend. A beautiful valley lies to the right below **4** and the plants now cover part of the road, so that we accustom ourselves to it and are inclined to call it a "field track" from now on. Every attempt to find a monopáti in the valley fails on account of walls or scrub, and so we remain on our "field track" which describes a long arc to the right before running on level ahead, through the wide, fertile plain, embedded between the two areas of hills. At the end of the plain is a **domed church**

0.40

5. Shortly after, we come to a fork above which lies our

next goal: a pass with a barrel-roofed chapel. It would be quicker to turn left and climb up to the chapel from here.

Anyone looking for a pleasant spot for a rest should go 200 m right and then up left, without a trail, to a wall which runs parallel to the valley below and immediately above a path. You pass through a hollow with some old, shady olive trees **6**. *The whole thing is perfected by a steady, pleasant breeze. We carefully choose a tree with a view of the sea. A wonderful place to open our retsina. The way to the main track leads below a fenced garden.*

1.00   Soon we arrive up at the **chapel** with its barrel roof and can make out another chapel (with a flat roof) **7** on the next ridge. Leaving the dirt track for a while, we take a short cut over a mule track, going right past a farmhouse up to the chapel. The chóra is now visible again from the top. Paros is so close, you think you are looking across a wide river **8**. We move on down and find another old mule track to the right of the dirt track. Don't head towards the harbour at the asphalt road, but bear *left* – past the ceme-

1.25   tery. We are soon in **Antiparos**, on a road which leads past a wonderful platía with a kafeneion and a eucalyptus tree.

If you want to have a look at the walled, Venetian town centre, or Kastro, head straight on through the only gateway and you will notice how much friendlier it is from within: with steps and much larger windows than on the outside, from where possible enemies had to be repelled.

Keeping right (towards the campsite) on the way out of
1.45   Kastro, head on through the dunes to the **beach.** Here, a sign draws your attention to pioneering days of old: "Nudist beach since the 70's". Today you can swim as you please, enjoying the sea which is as calm as a large swimming pool. The laziness of the other bathers soon catches on. To round it all off, a van selling cool drinks drives directly onto the beach.

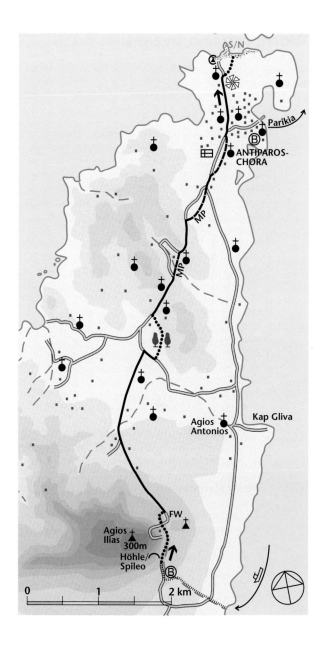

㉚ Along the Old Byzantine Road

*A walk of four hours which runs along
the old, medieval road connecting the two
coasts for part of the way and rewards
us with several sandy beaches at the end.*

There is an hourly **bus** from Parikía up through the mountains to **Léfkes**. Straight after arriving, you can imagine spending a lazy day, lost in thought, in one of the two tavernas with a magnificent view. Another time, perhaps! So we set off into the village which curves around the large church with its twin towers like an amphitheatre. After a wide left bend, which slopes gently downhill at the end, we come across a kafeneion. We turn right here and ask again, just to be on the safe side, for the small church of Agios Nikolaos hidden in a grove, below which the road

AWT 0.00   **forks 1**. We now rely on the yellow route sign, not really requiring any further directions. This is the old road which leads from the harbour of Pisso Livádi to Léfkes, formerly the largest town on the island, and on across the whole island as far as Parikía. **2 3**

Beyond the straits lies Naxos with Mt. Zeus, at 1001 m the highest mountain on the Cyclades, and, to the fore, the peak of Mt. Kéfalos **4** with its monastery. You cross over a

0.20   **bridge**, climbing uphill and, at the foot of the mountain,
0.45   arrive in **Prodromos**, the first of three villages on the plain.

▶ We could forego our picnic today and have lunch in the shady garden of the taverna "Tsitsánis" instead! The tavern lies unobtrusively on the main square.

Afterwards you walk right below the square, along the concrete road through the village, then left to the main road, going right here for 250 m to a chapel **5**. Take the dirt track

1.05   up left to **Marpissa**, which is crowned by a red-tiled dome. (Bus stop).

Alternative: the real enthusiasts who want to go on to the monastery of Agios Antónios on **Kéfalos**, should first head along the roadway, past the three windmills. The concrete road (later a dirt track) forks below the sparsely vegetated peak. Walk up right to the reservoir, turning off left just before onto the wonderful old path up to the monastery. It is paved with marble slabs and lined with thujas. From Marpissa

you will need 25 minutes to the summit. The outside of the monastery **6** has been renovated, but the church itself is closed. Ancient frescoes in the cupola are visible through the window. The site was originally occupied by a Venetian fortress which was captured by the Turks in 1537. This marked the beginning of Turkish rule over the island.

Those who prefer to go for a swim, should stroll leisurely through the attractive village of Marpissa towards the sea. On the outskirts (next to Hotel Afendakis) is a barrel-roofed chapel where you cross the main road and wander on a small road down along the stream. Here there are several dovecote towers and, in a hollow, you come across a collection of fallen-in houses **7**. Turning left here, you take the dirt track leading uphill which then becomes a footpath. You cross the main road at a hollow and, 50 m further ahead on the right, find a concrete road which leads to the sea. We soon arrive at the sandy bay of

1.40   **Pounda** **8** with club activity. If you want to head on, go directly along the shore, past two more small sandy bays,

2.15   to **Golden Beach**, where there are also several tavernas. This is the most beautiful beach on Paros. The **busses** back to Parikía (three-quarters of an hour's journey) leave 500 m behind the sea front.

> *Alternative:* from **Pounda** you can reach the peace and quiet of **Livádi** in under twenty minutes by heading along the coast, then passing the wide, sandy bay of Logaras (tavernas, tamarisks, no sunshades), and take the bus from there. Not bad either!

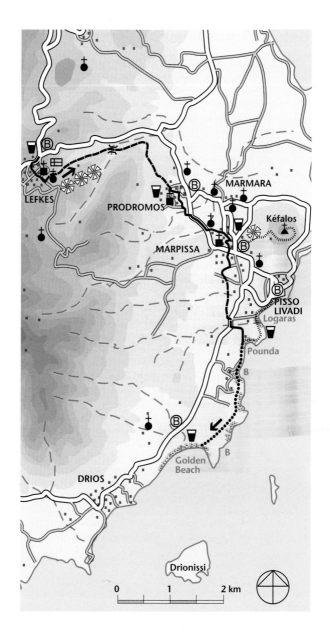

LEFKES

PRODROMOS

MARMARA

Kéfalos

MARPISSA

PISSO
LIVADI

Logaras

Pounda

B

B

Golden
Beach

DRIOS

Drionissi

0   1   2 km

Below Agios Ilias

> *A route of four to five hours through karst-type uplands on the eastern side of the Marpissa ridge, the main axis through the island, and down onto the lovely coastal plain around Aliki. There are no tavernas en route!*

AWT 0.00 You keep right on the way into the village of **Léfkes** ❶ and stroll up a slight incline. Having passed an imposing classicistic edifice on the right, you bear right in front of the supermarket and climb up some steps to the road, fol-

0.12 lowing it left at first. It leads us past a **chapel** ❷ from 1993 and a circular reservoir (both on the left) up to a plateau. Below left is the large church of Léfkes with a cluster of houses around it. You see another chapel on a hill to the right and then the town is behind you.

250 m after the chapel, we turn left off the road which heads towards the mast-topped mountain (Ag. Ilias). A

0.20 gently ascending **stone path** ❸, running parallel to the road, leads us further to the right. We wander straight on

0.25 at the fork, **crossing** the road again. The way now continues up low gradient (sign: Kaparos). We are now surrounded by agricultural land with a blue-domed monastery ❹ in the centre, like in an oasis. Through some

0.40 dense trees we soon come upon **Moni Agiou Ioannou Kaparos.**

> *The monastery is privately owned and no longer inhabited. If there is someone around with the key, it is possible to enter the tiny courtyard and take a look inside the church. 1646, the year of its foundation is inscribed above the doorway. The exquisite iconostasis with its magnificent stone carvings is worth a closer look. Then there are home-made wine and olives in the monastery courtyard.*

> *If no-one is there, you can sit at the marble table beneath the walnut tree in front of the monastery, sipping tap-water instead of wine and gathering your strength for the climb ahead.*

This begins at a bend, 30 m before the entry to the monastery, where you walk right into the countryside. A monopáti bypasses the hollow, leading around a shallow right

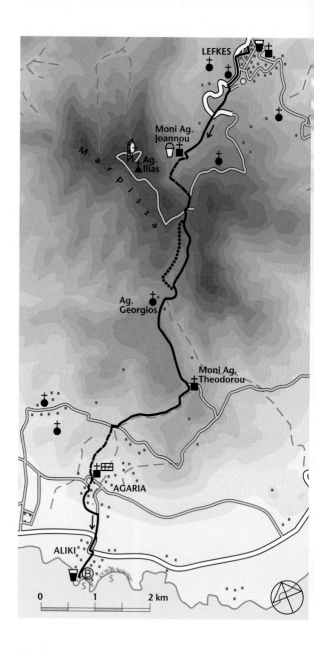

LEFKES

Moni Ag.
Joannou

Ag.
Ilias

Marpissa

Ag.
Georgios

Moni Ag.
Theodorou

AGARIA

ALIKI

0   1   2 km

bend before climbing uphill. You go straight on at the fork (red arrow) and wander up an incline. Red dots and a cairn lead the way until the path becomes a roadway. Turning right at the fork, you come back onto the original

1.00 **dirt road.** You bear right along it and, six minutes later, reach the pass in the middle of a barren, treeless landscape. At the pass you take the middle road going straight ahead (red dots). The blue dome of a barrel-roofed church **5** and two routes leading to it are visible below: you either take the easy way along the dirt road with the better view or, in true hiking manner, walk down right into the hollow along the rather difficult, stony trail.

1.30 Both the **Georgios chapel** and the cistern below are locked. On one side is a memorial to a resistance fighter who was executed in 1944. We head south along a high dirt road **6**, past a few poor houses with a pack of barking

1.55 dogs, to **Moni Agii Theodori.**

The convent was built in 1928 and may be visited by ladies attired in skirts from 10 to 12 a.m. and 3 to 5 p.m. The way continues to the right above the convent, though now amidst lovely trees, vineyards and barley fields. The new dirt road may not be the dream of the Cycladic hiker, but there is a fine view across to Antiparos. The dirt road

2.20 joins onto a **road** running **at an angle** to it below. Here you have to go right for some 150 m, then left (red dots) onto a monopáti halfway up the mountainside **7**, trekking on towards the sea. The path is somewhat overgrown – it is probably only still used by hunters. Below the blue-

2.40 **domed church** of Agaria, we parade past the war memorial
3.00 and bear right to the harbour of **Aliki 8**. Here you can have something to drink in the shade of bamboo-covered roofs or jump straight into the water. The bus leaves directly from the harbour. Length about 11 km.

㉜ **Between the Bays**

*Paros has two large natural harbours
which helped it to prosperity in antiquity.
This traversal of eleven kms from the bay of
Naoussa to the bay of Parikía takes five
hours and leads through hill country below
the mountain Profitis Elias, past two large
monasteries. Take your lunch with you for a
pleasant break in the monastery courtyard!*

AWT 0.00 From the **bus station** in **Naoussa**, follow the course of the stream uphill and cross the main road at the end of the village ten minutes later. A dirt road (signpost "Saraki-niko") leads into the hill country. You take the roadway

0.20 right **1** ahead of the **fork**.

The road straight ahead leads to Maráthi (㉝).

The monastery of St. Andrew stands in solitary splendour on the slope above the plain. To the left, the way is lined by barley fields, to the right it is karstic. You go left (*not* to Sarakiniko) 100 m after the turn-off to the refuse site, down to a loose collection of houses. Then left at the end (at hotel "Petres") and right straight after (Protoria sign) onto a rocky slope with a fork **2**. Here you bear left, turning right ahead before going straight on at the right bend of

0.45 the grey dirt road, directly past a **house 3** and onto a narrow path, above which there is a recently built chapel. This path joins onto a wide roadway which you follow down to the right. Heading on between houses and gardens, you arrive at the main road and turn left.

After the petrol station, you have to stay on the road for

1.00 200 m. Then go left up a **gravel road** on the edge of a tree nursery, right onto the second dirt track and on to a farmhouse over the flat.

Passing though barley fields, vineyards and a magnificent olive grove **4**, you come to a partly dilapidated windmill from 1869, whose interior can also be viewed. Above left in an aisle we now discover the hidden monastery **5**, to which the mill, the farmhouse in between as well as the monastery on the opposite slope all belong. We soon arrive

1.20 up at **Loggovardas Monastery**.

*The monastery courtyard is surrounded by a large block
of monks' cells. The number of monks living in the mon-*

astery has dropped from thirty to six today. Established in 1657, the monastery stood practically empty around 1800 and was later reoccupied in 1825. Only men can visit it. A monk born as "John" in England who became "Yiannis" in Greece, shows us around a few rooms such as the painting studio, the library and the kitchen. In the meanwhile, the women have waited an hour outside, but are then also invited to some lukumia, very sweet pieces of jelly dusted with icing sugar.

We now go left of the graveyard and the chapel, down across the valley, to the monastery on the opposite slope **6**. First along the paved track and then along the new roadway. At the end of the row of trees at a right angle ahead, we continue along the now barely visible monastery track to the main road. A solitary, very windswept tree points the way. This used to form the main link between the two monasteries. Cross swiftly over the road back onto the overgrown monopáti on the other side which leads up to the monastery.

1.45 **Taxiarchon Monastery** belongs to Loggovardas Monastery opposite and is not inhabited. Pigeons have taken it over, so the stone bench in front of the monastery is not such a good place to sit. We are better off taking a leisurely break under the shady tree in the middle of the monastery, with a view of the bay of Naoussa and the little church on the islet of Analipsi.

Our route continues on below the monastery, along the foothills of Mt. Profitis Elias. The pigeons are happy to have the walls back to themselves. We bear left twice along a roadway leading round the mountain. The bays of Parikía and Naoussa can now both be seen simultaneously. There is a chapel above us on the left and another to the right of the road **7**.

1.55 Beyond the chapels in a **right-hand bend** of the dirt road, an overgrown, and thus easily overlooked path along the slope forks to the *left*. We follow it, clearing branches out of the way, along

2.05   some dry-stone walls to a **twin chapel** 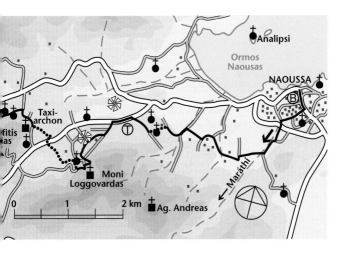. If you look, you will find a lion's paw in marble set into the wall.

Having crossed the road further on down, we find to path five metres along to the right, whose left wall used to carry water. 200 m further on, we come across a wide road, running at a right angle to the wall.

> *Alternative:* if you want to visit the sparse remains of the **Apollon Temple of Delion**, you turn *right* here and follow the bend round, arriving at a farmhouse with the usual yapping dogs. Just to the right of it is a footpath leading to the road on the opposite slope. Directly below the barrel-roofed chapel, up on the slope, is an entrance marked "dead end" which takes us uphill. Here you bear left along the dirt track. Little remains of the temple itself; but the panoramic view across to Delos and Mykonos makes the detour really worthwhile. The way descends from here to Parikía.

Without visiting the ruins, we pace quickly along the wide road through the fields. At the end there are some 150 m of asphalt before we can swim out into the evening
2.35   sun in the **bay of Parikía.**

㉝ The Marble Quarries of Marathi

This strenuous six-hour hike can be broken off after four and a half hours. It leads through rather quiet areas of Paros, past two monasteries, to the famous, ancient marble quarries. There are no tavernas en route. A torch should perhaps be taken along for visiting the underground quarries.

It's best to meet after a substantial breakfast on the road along the seafront of **Parikía**, below the retaining walls of **AWT 0.00** the **Constantine Church** with its blue dome. We march cheerfully westwards to the church with the twin towers and then down the small ramp ■ to the square. We follow the road right, which winds up over wide bends, cross the **0.10 main road** at the bridge and go straight on at the other side. At the first fork we bear *right* and *left* at the second. The houses of Kalogeria remain to the right of the road, and there are (still) fields on the left. Luxurious holiday houses with huge rubblestone walls cry out for admiration. One (with an outside staircase) lies directly across our path – we go round it on the left. Below left in the valley, a petite female artist works on huge blocks of marble in the tradition of the ancient Parian school of sculpture. Bearing **0.20** right at the fork, we wander past a **chapel** with a flat roof out into the countryside.

A farm track leads up to a dirt road. You walk 100 m along it to the left and then right, uphill. The slope becomes fairly steep halfway up the mountain, so progress is not as fast as down below at the harbour. Further on, we come to some power lines ■ on the path. This leads down to a **0.45 fence** on the floor of a valley. 20 m *ahead* of it, we turn off left under the cables, where black arrows now take over the leadership. The picturesque route sign-posted as "poet's **0.55** walk" above the gorge ■ leads up to a superb **olive grove.** This will be the only one today, so we are happy to sit on a wall and rest awhile. Above the grove, the track stretches straight on ahead to the uninhabited hermitage of Agios Dimitris ■. But we go right before, along the dry bed, past the washing troughs of a shabby hamlet and then up left to the old, rather overgrown monopáti, which we

follow to the right. It joins onto a concrete road which
1.20 leads up to the huge, battlemented convent of **Moni Thapsanon** from 1939 **5**, to which only ladies wearing skirts
are admitted. We carry on to the left along the dirt road.
After 100 m, you turn right onto a dirt track and soon see
1.25 a house with a **fence**. 40 m *before,* you force your way down
the slope on the right onto a monopáti, clearing the way
as you go. On the right is a wide, high-lying valley and,
above it, the Marpissa mountain range, the backbone of
the island, with the mast-topped peak of Agios Ilías, 755
m. At the fork, we walk right into the valley and see our
next goal, the large, dazzling white edifice of the monas-
1.40 tery of Minas which dominates the plain **6**. In the **creek**,
where there are several beehives, you hike on left past the
cistern, continuing above the dry bed to the chapel
1.50 and, from there, into the almost deserted **village** of
Vounia. Quick strides can be taken along the dirt track
which follows. The monastery draws ever closer: having
climbed up left from the hollow, you now stand directly
in front of the solidly built walls of the monastery of
2.05 **Agios Minas** (p. 122).

> *Our arrival was noticed some time ago. A strange old man
> guards the empty monastery. At one time, there were four-
> teen monks. Now you only meet the friendly man who
> makes bagpipes and gladly (in exchange for a small offer-
> ing) invites you to some wine or water. He once worked in
> Canada and has also travelled around a good deal. Sat at
> the stone table in the shade, there is barely time to draw
> breath in between all the chat. The 300-year old church
> is rather bare inside, but the tiny courtyard with an arbour
> and cypresses is very picturesque in comparison.*

The next part of our trek is the continuation of the previous stony path. It leads up over countless zigzags to the
2.15 **quarries.** What we are looking for lies at the foot of the
opposite slope.

> *The **ancient marble quarries** are two long ramps **7** of
> about four metres in width which lead down into the
> mountain. The prized marble was quarried and pulled up
> on the ramps from far below. Parian marble is the most
> translucent in the world, still allowing light to pass
> through it at a thickness of 35 mm. Two tunnels are acces-
> sible and are connected diagonally with each other below.
> It is possible to climb down from the carving into the*

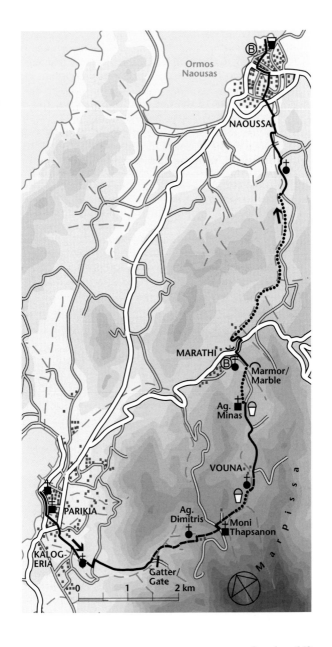

Ormos
Naousas

NAOUSSA

MARATHI
Marmor/
Marble

Ag.
Minas

VOUNA

Ag.
Dimitris
Moni
Thapsanon

PARIKIA

KALOG-
ERIA

Gatter/
Gate

Marpissa

0   1   2 km

tunnel on the right (only in twos and with a torch!), cross below, and reappear at the left opening forty minutes later.

2.20   The way to the **road** leads along recently laid marble.

Short cut: there are busses from Marathi to Parikía or Léfkes.

The next leg of the way first leads right for 200 m along the road, then bears down left ahead of a concrete works onto a concrete road, which ends at the bottom of a valley. This dry bed **8** leads to Naoussa, winding harmoniously over the terrain. You can stroll on carefree, easily finding

2.55   your bearings. At the **pumping station** you should remain
3.10   in the creek so as to please the eye. When a **path** crosses the dry bed, you take the dirt track uphill on the right and can soon see Naoussa ahead. A small church on the right of the track gives its blessing for the last stretch.

3.45   We arrive on the outskirts of **Naoussa** along dirt tracks and, soon after, proudly sail into the **harbour**, "making fast" in one of the tavernas, after this 15 km walk.

Santoríni

This volcanic island differs entirely from the other islands of the Cylades. It took on its present appearance in the wake of the explosion beneath what had been a circular limestone island. A layer of ejected pumice tuff up to sixty metres in height was deposited on what was left of the island. There are hardly any trees outside the built-up areas. Vineyards dominate the landscape to which roads and trails provide good access. For this reason secluded hikes are not possible everywhere. The hewn monopátia edged with back volcanic stone are typical of Santoríni.

A good map of the island is available from some shops (1:50 000, Harms Verlag, Germany).

㉞ Cliffhanger

This is the classical Santoríni trek:
three hours along the verge of the precipice
with spectacular views and a wonderful
picnic spot!

If you don't want to arrive in Oía until sunset, there is
sufficient time if you set off at 2 p.m. The tour begins at
AWT 0.00 the Archaeological **Museum** of **Thíra**, leads past the well-
known vantage points and soon offers a view of Imerovígli
1. First we stroll through Fírostefani, then on past the large
convent of Agios Nikolaos (a tour is possible), to Imerovígli **2** **3**, we take the dirt track
along the edge of the crater. Beyond a hollow, where there
0.55 is a graveyard, the road climbs gently before **forking** at a
hotel complex. Our later route continues along to the
right.

★
> *It takes five minutes down to the left to reach St. Anto-*
> *nius Chapel **4**, a place to while, the likes of which are*
> *but seldom on the Cyclades. Everything is already pre-*
> *pared for us: tables, a shady eucalyptus tree, a cool cave,*
> *a tap and even a WC hut. The small bottle of retsina is*
> *pulled out of the rucksack with contentment and our eyes*
> *wander over the shimmering, blue inland sea…*
>
> *The island of Volcano, which rose up a mere 300 years*
> *ago from the almost 400 m-deep caldera, lies peacefully*
> *in the centre of the crater. This landscape was formed by*
> *the largest natural catastrophe in the history of mankind.*
> *The volcano, originally 1600 m high, erupted around*
> *1530 BC, then collapsed inwards. In one fell swoop it*
> *destroyed civilisation on Strongili – "the circular one", as*
> *the island was then known – and proabably also, as a*
> *result of tidal waves, Minoan civilisation on Crete. The*
> *remains of this civilisation can be admired in Akrotiri.*

Unwillingly, we leave this belvedere and climb back up to
the main track, before passing a dilapidated church ahead.
1.10 The church of **Profitis Elias 5** stands almost at the top of
the mountain. After walking down over a somewhat
1.20 rough, stony path **6** along the precipice to the **road**, you
follow the latter for some 250 m.

At the cantina, known for its freshly-squeezed oranges, is
an attractive mule track leading uphill to Negolo Vounó.

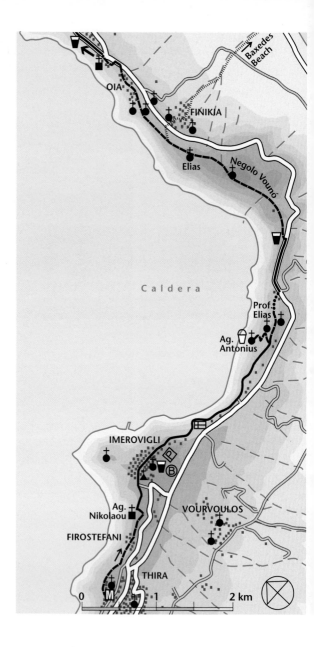

Baxedes
Beach

OIA

FINIKIA

Elias

Negolo Vounó

Caldera

Prof.
Elias

Ag.
Antonius

IMEROVIGLI

VOURVOULOS

Ag.
Nikolaou

FIROSTEFANI

THIRA

0   1   2 km

1.45 A **chapel 7** with a superb view of the northern part of Santoríni awaits us on the next peak. The way now continues down over lava to the village of Finikía, past another chapel **8** which today bears the name of the prophet Elias.

> *Alternative:* anyone wanting to go for a **swim,** should go right over the hill 250 m after the chapel of Elias, heading downhill on the right of the water tank, across the road and down into the peaceful village of **Finikía,** with its courtyards and narrow lanes. Continuing on below the church, you turn left next to an overgrown footpath, out of the eroded valley and straight on to the sea. To get from here to Oía, you either follow the descriptions in (㉟, in the opposite direction) or take the bus.

2.05 On the outskirts of Oía, you are initially disappointed by the rumbling ensuing from a **factory building.** It is the desalination plant which supplies the precious water for our daily, morning shower. Heading on over a hillside path, past enticing swimming pools, we come to the road next to "Oía Market", and follow it for a short stretch. We

2.10 bear left up the steps from the **Church of St. George** and cross the churchyard to the main road through Oía. A few minutes along to the right is the taverna "Blue Sky" which offers a magnificent view back along the way we've come. Some time later, we follow the stream of tourists headed, like us, along the main way to "Sunset Point".

35 Beachcomber

Like beachcombers we wander in six hours from Oía on the east coast, past many attractive bathing spots. The trek can be broken off in Imerovígli.
The first part of the hike is also an attractive way of getting from Oía to the beach.

AWT 0.00 This trek begins to the right of the dustbins opposite **"Oía
Market"** 1, where you go down the mule track 2. You may
have trouble with the broken stones, but less with the
orientation. The path leads down towards the sea between
vineyards. Heading left along the dirt track and turning off
it to the right after 200 m, will bring you straight to the
0.30 taverna "Paradisos" on the **road.** Here there are three
taverns to choose from, or you can proceed straight on
down to the black and white **Beach of Baxedes** 3, drag
your feet through the sand and drift on in a northerly
direction. Soon you find yourself alone with the bizarrely
1.00 shaped pumice cliffs 4 5. There are a few **tamarisks** on
the beach – perhaps you'll be lucky and the places in the
shade are still free. Further on, the head of **Cape Koloumpos** pushes into the sea 6, but you have *already* scrambled
1.20 up right, over fallen dry-stone walls, to the **marker post.**
The mountain of Kókkino Voúno lies above, Folégandros,
Síkinos and Ios are lined up like pearls in the sea – and all
around is the scent of thyme.

We then use the dirt road for a few metres before going
down left, through the dry bed, back to the water where
there are all sorts of flotsam and jetsam – perfect for the
beachcomber! A row of windmills, which we will pass later
on, is visible on the hill ahead. Over some steps in the red
1.55 cliffs, we arrive in the small **fishing port** where Capt.
Jannis, who can be rather grumpy at times, runs a cantina.
Not only for the fishermen!

We continue on up to the main road, cross it and head on
without a trail, accompanied by prickly pears, along the
foot of the mountain to the windmills. En route we will
2.10 come across **two chapels** 7.

On closer inspection, the "windmills" 8 turn out to be new, four-storey holiday homes. The building law permits two extra floors because of the windmill shape.

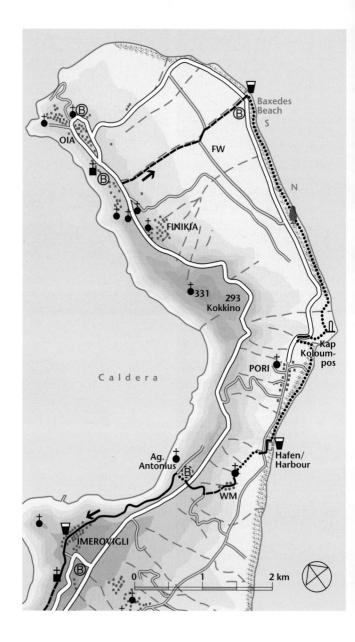

OIA

Baxedes
Beach
S

FW

N

FINIKIA

331
293
Kokkino

Caldera

Kap
Koloumpos

PORI

Hafen/
Harbour

Ag.
Antonius

WM

IMEROVIGLI

0   1   2 km

Above the holiday-mills, you struggle uphill through tangled scrub, going slightly left, to the **mountain road** which you follow along to the main road and a bus stop. On the other side, a worn trail leads over the mountain ridge to the caldera route. If you walk left, you soon arrive on the outskirts of **Imerovígli.** Here, you can either take the bus or have something to eat before strolling along the "promenade", past **Fírostefani** with its quiet, attractive taverns, to **Thíra.** Route length about 13 km.

2.40

3.00

3.35

㊱ Erosion

The eroded valleys, as typical for Santoríni as the caldera precipice, are little known. From the fort of Pírgos you have a view over the largest of the valleys. Our route is quickly planned: we will climb down into the next valley, wander through the gorge in the village of Vóthonoas towards the airport and on to bathe in Kamarí. We should schedule two and a half to three hours.

The Perissa bus takes you to **Pírgos**, the capital of the island until 1800. You stroll through the old, winding lanes up to the Venetian fortress. Here your gaze can roam far over Santoríni. Before descending, you should note the obvious, disruptive concrete factory below the town, facing in the direction of Thíra, as you will have to pass it later on.

AWT 0.00   Below the fortress is a small **obelisk** – a military memorial. You walk west in the alley below and come across a church **1** 50 m further on. The path leads downhill to the right from here, under a flying buttress and right at the fork down to a concrete ramp which joins onto a road. Going right along it for 40 m, you take another concrete ramp down to the left. Soon the ramp has become a clean, plastered winegrowers' path, dug into the ground and pleas-

0.10   ant to walk along. The **road** (left, the concrete factory) hardly bothers us as, ten metres on to the right, our path continues on down into the eroded valley (red dot). The typical, black Santoríni surface **2** accompanies us until we have left the vineyards and enter the pumice gorge. Prickly pears stand on the wayside of the deepening eroded valley. For centuries the winter rains have been filing away at the pumice deposits which measure up to a thickness

0.20   of 60 m. The outskirts of **Vóthonoas** have a rather pitiful and dilapidated appearance. Many of the typical cave dwellings are still in ruins after the earthquake of 1956. Some 3000 houses were destroyed on the island at the time. The caves are ideal for their inhabitants – cool in the summer and warm in the winter, though unfortunately not very stable.

Alternative: eight minutes later in the next valley on the left, you come across a church in a cave, **Panagiatis Sergeinas**, with a small bell cot, room to celebrate and some cisterns .

The upper part of church consists of a large chamber hewn into the rock, which acted as a hideout during pirate raids in the Middle Ages. It is locked; those interested should look for the warden in the valley beforehand.

Just before the village is the large church of Panagia with a huge eucalyptus tree; bear round it and turn into the small lane. Here you come across a church with six bell cots and, further on, a neo-classical house. You then head downhill before turning down right at the crossing into the main alleyway. Above left, the domed church with the immense belfry bearing nine bell cots overlooks the village. Having seen enough, you go down the lane , past some more cave dwellings , to the **end of the**

0.30 **village**, and wander on over numerous bends out of the eroded valley. On the right is a twin church in a cave, dug

0.45 out of the slope; shortly after, you cross the **main road** next to a taverna before trudging slowly ahead through the

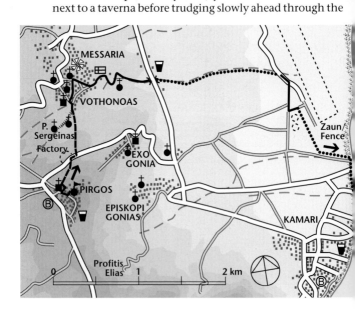

fine sand of a dry bed 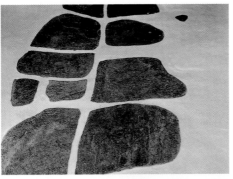 towards the sea. Since roads have been built, the dry creeks are only used by hikers from abroad and mules. You later follow the cement road right and, 200 m before the airport fence, turn right onto a dirt track. After a few hundred metres you come to a sign with "horse-riding" written on it and two threshing circles behind it. Bear left here, then right without a path to the next dry bed, thus detouring the airport. The creek leads

1.40   directly to the **sandy beach** of **Kamarí,** where the other bathers are surprised to see our white, dusty shoes.

From here it is still another half an hour to the bus, which leaves for Thíra once an hour.

㊲ Ancient Théra – Never on a Monday!

Along with Akrotíri and Delos, the ancient site of Théra, founded in the 8th century BC, is the main archaeological sight on the Cylcades. This trek leads in four to five hours over the pass of Mt. Messavounó. I hiked this route for the first time on a Monday: both the ruins and the kiosk were closed and a bleak, empty car park the reward at the summit. Other than on a Monday, you should set off with enough time to accommodate the opening hours.

To **Empório** (well worth a visit) it is a half-hour bus journey: you should try to sit on the right of the bus which is sometimes overcrowded in the morning.

*The houses of the **kastro**, the old town higher up, are joined together on the outside like a castle and a linked by a maze of narrow lanes within. You enter through two covered passages and, with luck, leave the same way. Fortunately, little has been done to attract tourists. Beyond the town you can visit the ruins of a Venetian tower-house.*

To find where our trek continues later on, you should first find your bearings on a terrace below the kastro (at the exit marked "1831"). On the outskirts of the town, at the foot of the mountain to the south-east, there is a church with three vaults in the fields **2**. Approximately 80 m to the right of it is our later route.

After descending the steps from the terrace to the chapel in the hollow, we bear right, then 200 m down the slope

AWT 0.00 before turning left between two barrel-roofed **storehouses** **1** onto a narrow roadway leading up a slight incline. 100 m ahead on the left is the torso of a windmill. The road narrows into a deeply embedded monopáti. On the left in the middle of the fields is the three-vaulted church of Agios Taxiarchis **2**, which we could see from above.

0.05 After having turned onto the **roadway** which comes down from the left, you leave it again at the second right-hand bend, bearing *left* onto a worn path which runs on to a retaining wall. Going along here, you come to a house with a rural chapel **3**. After a few steps, you cross the dirt road (there is a transformer box on an electricity mast here)

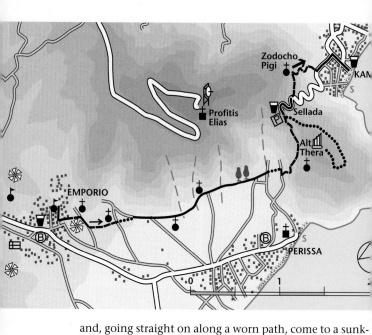

and, going straight on along a worn path, come to a sunken, well-tended monopáti, along which you head up right

0.12 to a **group of houses** on the right of the track. This becomes a dirt track and you continue along it, going left at the fork and then straight on. Brushing past a chapel, you hike left along the foot of the mountain **4** **5**.

Perissa stretches along the coast to the right; the island of Anaphi is visible beyond in the distance. Planes fly straight towards the rock on which Ancient Théra lies. If you take a closer look, you will discover a small chapel, built daringly into the rock.

0.30 Now we are at the **end of the valley** below; our path uphill **6** lies on the right slope. We keep to the right over the level ground, then climb over a monopáti, reaching a metal sign after 50 m along the road: now the ascent can begin.

The track up to Sellada, as the pass is known, is fairly steep but can be covered in half an hour. There is generally a strong wind blowing here, but there is an interesting view

1.00 over the built-up plain of Perissa. A **canteen** on wheels awaits us above. But never on a Monday **7**.

*If you want to visit **Ancient Théra**, you should be there by 1.30 p.m., as visitors have to leave the site by 2.30 p.m. There are well-preserved remains of buildings dating from the Ptolemaic era around 250 BC. The position of the town and the fact that both the agora and the theatre face the sea are particularly impressive.*

Anyone itching to go for a swim, can take a minibus from here to the coast. But, never on a Monday.

The route for pleasure-seekers, who should be fairly steady on their feet, leads to a path heading away from the road at the third right-hand bend. (Otherwise you can reach Kamarí via the road.)

1.15   The superb hiking trail runs high above Kamarí along the mountain. Later on, you reach the chapel of **Zoodocho Pigi** ("life-giving source") **8** over some steps.

A picture-book site, such as is only to be found on the Cyclades: a stone table for the visitors of the parish fair and bells hanging in the branches. There is heavenly peace up here, only a short way above the hectic of Kamarí. Though the life-giving source in the cave, being barred, cannot fulfil its purpose.

1.30   The road is paved from here, leading down over hair-pin bends to the black sands of **Kamarí.**

We can take our time with the journey back as the last bus doesn't leave until 11 p.m. in summer.

㊳ Akrotíri

After visiting the world-famous Minoan excavations, you climb up to the village of Akrotíri, wandering first along the edge of the crater before reaching a pleasant place to stop, in front of a chapel on the flat, seaward side of the island. Then it's off for a swim. You have the choice between a practically empty and an organised beach.

Take the bus to the **Akrotíri excavations.** In high summer the archaeological site is open until 7 p.m., so you could also visit it after the trek during this time.

The excavations of Akrotíri **1** *are one of the greatest archaeological sensations of the 20th century. The uncovered parts are 3500 years old and the two layers below are said to be as much as 8000 years old. A free plan is available at the ticket office. Inside, the important sites are supplied with descriptions and reproductions of the frescoes found there. The finds are stored in wooden cabinets, so you feel almost like an archaeologist yourself. The plaster cast of the famous wooden bed is exhibited at the end of the tour. It burned during the hot rain of pumice stone and was only preserved as an imprint. The measurements give an approximate idea of the size of the people of the period.*

AWT 0.00 The trek begins at the **attendant's hut** in the car park above. From here, a worn path leads left to a terrace. You go along the retaining wall until you cross a monopáti, which winds along the foot of the slope. Going right, you walk through the floor of a valley **2** up to a road, turn right here to the main road and then up left to the bus stop in

0.15 **Akrotíri.**

Bearing left uphill from here to the neo-classical school, you continue in the direction of the beak of the bird sat on the monument. Anyone wanting to have a quick look at the narrow streets of the renovated kastro, should take the steps on the left.

Going round the church to the right from the steps, you head up to the road on which you remain up to the hairpin bend. Here there is a lane leading off uphill to the left. Take the first lane on the left, going past an attractive,

lowered chapel and a tight cluster of houses. At the end of the village is another chapel on the left. Here you go right along the concrete road up to a fork (Minimarket), and then left. Continuing on through the next group of houses, you turn right onto a track which is lined by stone walls on both sides and come past an attractive **villa 3**. Ahead, at the next bend, we have a tremendous view of the "inland sea" and the three towns Oía, Thíra and mountainside Pírgos, above which – as on every Cycladic island – Prophet Elias keeps watch from his mountain top.

0.25

The mule track leads us further, almost without any effort on our part, before we go 50 m along a road to a twin chapel. There is a sign leading down a stepped path to **Panagia Kinisi 4**. We bear left ahead of the paled gate of this pilgrimage church onto the mule track **5** towards the lighthouse on Cape Akrotíri. Below the mountain top to the south-west is a chapel – our resting spot!

0.35

You wander on over the flat, between the vines lying on the ground. Perhaps we should try some of the island wine this evening! It grows so well here because the volcanic rock is particularly fertile and the pumice absorbs the dew, then releases it gradually. The grape harvest takes place as early as the end of August.

A dirt track crosses ahead and we follow it left for 60 m. At the left bend, we bear right onto a hewn path. Then there is another dirt track and we go left.

> *Alternative:* if you want to wander on to Cape Akrotíri, you have to climb down into the small eroded valley straight ahead. Turning right up ahead of a solitary tree, you follow some charming paths above the sea and reach the wonderfully old-fashioned lighthouse in 50 minutes.

Our main route aims towards the chapel on the rock. The dirt road offers little for the eye – just ordinary countryside **6**. Yet soon we come out of our visual depression: we walk up a few metres to the Taxiarchis (archangel) **chapel 7** and do something here for our spirtual welfare, for our eyes and against our thirst. Every drop of water from the cistern is blessed and poor eyesight restored by Saint Paraskeyí. Below the square, a wide landscape, in which several half-finished buildings have accumulated, opens up before us. A shady bank has been built for our siesta …

0.50

1.10	We speed on downhill over the dirt road towards the **sea** to the little frequented white sands of
1.20	"White Beach". Anyone looking for a more lively beach, should walk on over the cliffs to "**Red Beach**" ⬛. Despite the numerous sun-shades and sunbeds,
1.35	there is little in the way of cater-

ing. In the summer there are kaikis to take you on further or to "Black Beach" around the corner.

Over the red cliffs and then along the road you arrive back at the **bus stop.** Further down, at the sea front, is another bus stop where the waiting is more pleasant!

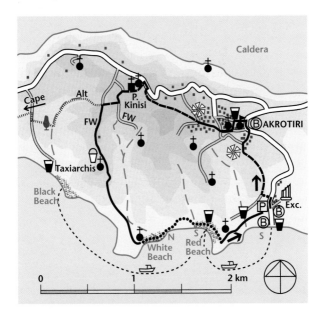

Schinoússa

Both from the map and from the sea this member of the "Small Cyclades" appears more rugged than it is in reality. A closer look reveals

gently rolling hills, meadows and even pasture land, large cisterns, small olive groves, vineyards and noticeably few chapels. The topography has always permitted the use of horse-drawn vehicles which has led to the fact that there are relatively few mule tracks.

39 Three Sandy Coves

The longest beaches are in the south below Chóra; we will visit three other small, isolated coves. There are no tavernas or serviceable cisterns on the trek. Three to four hours are needed to complete this eleven km circular route with very few inclines. Though several waist-high field walls have to be surmounted.

AWT

0.00   We begin on the north side of the village at the **bakery**, heading away from the houses, and turn down right after 80 m into the lovely countryside with numerous islands and islets floating in the sea beyond. After a cistern (right)

0.10   we go through a wide **gate**, bear left past the next cistern on the right and wander above a stony bay before continuing along the coast, either without a path or along

0.25   trails, and around the hill to the **bay of Psilí-Ámmos.** It is forbidden to anchor here as the electricity ring main, which now links the islands, runs along the sea floor. Thanks to this, the noisy diesel generators of earlier days have now become superfluous.

We head on over easily recognisable trails along the rocky coastline. Wide terraces allow a broader view up to the highest mountain of the Cyclades, Mt. Zeus on Naxos. The

0.40   next sandy beach, **Fikío Beach** is more to our liking!

The way heads inland at some ruins, passing to the left of

the vineyard and left at the end of a wall onto a mule track. After a few metres, we have to climb over a stone wall on the right and then walk along the edge of the fields towards the windmill. Having jumped nimbly over another two walls, we come to a mule track leading to an unsealed road.

0.55   We follow this left for 50 m before **turning off** right. Fairly soon the path stops in a dead end and we continue on

1.10   down without a trail to the small **sandy cove.** Well, wasn't it worth it? If you're lucky, you have the 21 m of sand alone to yourself.

We return by going back up to the roadway, turning right, then right again up an incline from the cistern. At the left bend we take the flagstone path to the right, and later head

1.40   up left without a trail though the field to the **windmill.** Inside the well-preserved mill, the technically interested will wonder why the millstones are so high up.

The village is reached by proceeding through the hollow without a trail, the antenna to your left, and then on

2.00   downhill to the road to **Schinoússa.**

▶ At the hotel "Anesis" you can purchase a decent map of the island (and enjoy a fantastic night view from one of the rooms over to Santoríni, starry sky included.)

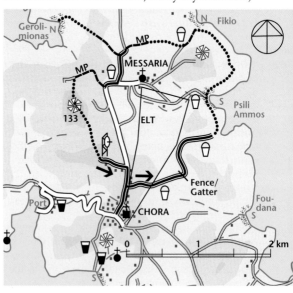

Sérifos

A massif of granite dominates the centre of the
island. The chóra, built half way up, looks down
over pleasant green slopes and beautiful sandy
bays. Not yet overrun, this island is the right
choice for hikers in search of calm as, for the most
part, it offers paths without a concrete surface.

⑩ The Chóra of Sérifos

This four-hour trek leads along the old paved path up to Chóra. The way heads on from the other side through a gentle, fertile landscape down to the dune-lined, sandy beach of Psíli Ammos.

AWT 0.00   The trek begins at the **pedestrian bridge**, directly on the beach of **Livádi**. You go up the road, turn right at the next large bridge and soon leave the cars behind you as the old stair-path forks right off the road after a few metres. Up on the outskirts of the village, there is a war memorial to the

0.30   right. Remaining on the wide path, you pass a **church** with a blue dome, from where you continue up to the right. Using the road for 50 m, you then take the stepped path on the right again. At the fork below the rock, bear left to

0.40   the attractive **platía** **2** with a church, two kafenía with shady tables and the austere, neo-classical town hall.

To the right of the town hall is a small lane **3** leading down which veers left 50 m ahead. Turn down right at an angle *before* the bus stop onto a track which leads out of Chóra **4**. You pass a group of houses and continue at the same height, ignoring a way leading down right to a cemetery. A superb track now begins. There is a bridge with a cistern **5** in the small valley ahead and dovecote towers along its slopes.

0.55   The paved track leads uphill to **two houses** on a hilltop, one of which is a chapel. We head on into the next valley where every herb of the Mediterranean sprouts at our feet, their scent exciting our nose. There is a chapel above to the right. After a bridge with a steel railing, we enter a hollow lane between dry-stone walls. The idyll must unfortunately be left behind after a mere 150 m and a way found uphill to the right without a trail **6**. Though goat herds have already cleared some tracks. Obviously with intent, as the view to Chóra, Livádi and the sea is fantastic. On the left above Livádi is a prominent, rocky cone-shaped peak, our next goal **7**. We look for a way in the hollow below the group of trees. A path runs down from the left between two field walls on the opposite slope. It is easy to walk along and is full of peppermint bushes in spring. You now need to look for a path which runs right, above the

hollow, the farmhouses remaining down below to your left. Hiking towards the sea, you soon find a mule track coming from the farmhouses on the left. Going right along

1.15 it, then right again, you reach a **bridge** above a valley strewn with oleander bushes. A few steps further and

1.20 you're in front of a **wall** directly below the cone.

The way to Psilí Ammos leads left, down along the right side of a small ravine, which you cross at some pools in the rock, then on past a farmhouse on the right and up to

1.35 a dirt road whose path you follow to the **bay of Psilí Ammos** ◪. Fine sand, dunes, tamarisks, two taverns – what more could you want? The landlady of the taverna has a tip for the way back: first left along the dirt road from the bay, but then left 100 m further on, up along an easily recognisable, worn trail. Now across the dirt road at the top before marching down through the dry creek, all the

2.00 way back to **Livádi.**

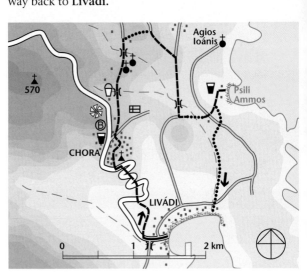

Sífnos

Two mountain ranges of marble divide this green, fertile island. The lush vegetation and the gentle incline of the many mule tracks still in use make Sífnos one of the favourite islands among Cyclades hikers. Along the trails in the charming landscape one encounters several large monasteries and numerous chapels. A precise map by John Burkett-Smith on a scale of 1:40 000 from 1995 is available from stationers' and card shops on Sífnos.

Panagía Chryssopigi 42

㊶ At the Foot of the Prophet

This four-hour route is easy to find and leads through a sparsely cultivated area to a valley at the foot of Profitis Elías. For relaxing at the end of the trek, taverna chairs on the sand and the beach of the quiet bay of Vathí await us.

You should find out the bus times from Vathí before starting out!

AWT 0.00 The day begins at the **memorial square** of Apollonía, at the passage next to the cake shop which leads into a narrow alleyway. You turn right 40 m ahead, up the stair-lane. The boutiques are still closed and the chairs of the tavernas upturned. A few people are already having their breakfast. Up at the other end of the stair-path, head right for a few metres along the asphalt road, leaving it again at the signpost to Katavati. You go left below the church of **Katavati** ■, then on past the hotel "Galini" and the

0.15 church of **Panagía Angelokísti**, in whose forecourt lies the beautiful epitaph of a pope. At the fork, 80 m further on, signposts point right towards Mt. Elias. You head straight on downhill over concrete, through an olive grove, to the bypass which you follow right for 50 m before climbing up some steps (sign "Elias"). Not much can go wrong from here, and there are blue marker dots into the bargain! The track you now use, lies on the slope opposite Mt. Elias.

0.35 In a hollow, the **trail** to Profitis Elias **forks** off to the right (see below). Later on, our route ■ bears right (arrow) below a chapel ■ into a valley where the Archangel and his

0.45 church, **Taxiarchis tis Skafis** ■, appear to us amidst some ruins. If it is open, you can see some beautiful, though badly damaged frescoes in the chancel, or bema. Some of the monastery terraces in the valley are planted with vines, watched over from above by the fortified monastery of the

1.00 Prophet Elias. Attractive steps lead on to the **pass** from where Mílos and Kímolos are visible.

From the saddle we are lead left uphill by a concrete path which then becomes a reddish scree track. Now you have to be careful: 30 m above a wall, a narrow path forks off the wider one to the left. We take the narrower of the two, which runs up above and parallel to the larger one, and

follow the contour lines, our eyes fixed on the white, domed church 5 which lies on the right, below the next peak. Blue dots and cairns line our route. A huge crevice is visible on the opposite slope. Which one of the Greek Gods raged here? The mule track brushes the walls on the left of the pass, and follows round the curves of the next hill, keeping at the same height. The track winds on ahead
1.30 through juniper bushes to the monastery of **Agios Niko-laos Tiaerina** in whose forecourt there is a faucet. If you don't want to wait and have your picnic under olive trees in twenty minutes time, the best place to stop for a rest is the roof of the toilet building. The day's goal, Vathí with its attractive bay, is visible down below. The way there begins between the monastery and the small building mentioned above, running down a slight incline. Soon another path coming down from the right joins onto our track. Some more blue dots appear, pointing the way ahead to the left. We stay left of the fissured mountain, moving on over broken stones and through juniper bushes. A prickly barricade has to be climbed over before you choose among the extremely pleasant sites to have a picnic in the walled fields ahead!

The well-marked track 6 leads down to the bay 7. In
2.10 **Vathí**, the taverna "Tsikali" 8 with its chairs on the sand awaits us! Even before ordering, we have taken off our shoes and removed the burs from our socks. Then the draught beer is brought.

The sandy beach is right next door. To reach the bus, you have to walk 100 m inland. The last bus leaves relatively early in the spring, and as late as midnight in the high season.

To Profitis Elías o Psilós ("The Tall One")

From the turn-off in the valley (AWT 0.35), you climb uphill for an hour, at first over a mountain trail (red dots) and later on a stair-path up to the fortress-like, deserted monastery. From here you have the most beautiful view across Sífnos and the islands surrounding it in the deep blue Aegean.

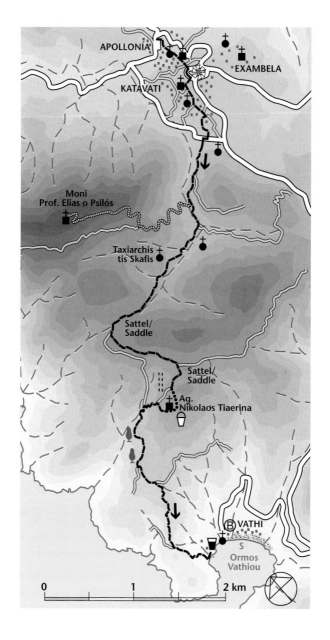

APOLLONIA

EXAMBELA

KATAVATI

Moni
Prof. Elias o Psilós

Taxiarchis
tis Skafis

Sattel/
Saddle

Sattel/
Saddle

Ag.
Nikolaos Tiaerina

Ⓑ VATHI

S
Ormos
Vathiou

0   1   2 km

⁴² Sífnos' Most Scenic Spot

An easy trek of three and a half hours from Apollonía to the church of Chryssopigi, "the" most scenic spot on the island. The route is easy to find and leads gently downhill all the way to the sea. Here there are attractive tavernas and a bathing beach!

You should find out the times of the return journey from Faros before starting out!

AWT 0.00 From between the cake shop and the map of the island on the **main square** of **Apollonía**, you walk 40 m to the main alley "Odos Prodou" which leads us up to the right (p. 190).

*30 m ahead of the large domed church is the flat-roofed church of **Ag. Fanorius** (1768) on the right with a picturesque forecourt and a series of ancient frescoes along the walls inside. It is open early in the morning.*

Level with the steps on the left is a high wall belonging to the school. Here we turn left onto the narrow path, first walking downhill then uphill, where it is somewhat overgrown, to the road. We continue on the other side between windmill ruins, aiming for the blue dome in the village of **Exambela**. Depending on ability, you arrive more or less

0.18 directly at the **blue-domed church** of St. Nicholas **1** which you pass on your left. Our way leads down right at the fork and then left a few metres further on. The sloping track first heads towards the sea, then right, past the remains of an ancient circular tower in the middle of a farm to the left of the track. The impressive ruin was built in the 3rd to 6th century BC without mortar using precisely hewn stones. There are still some 40 of these tower bases on the island; they served as places of refuge and for transmitting light signals.

You then reach the road and follow it left for some 220 m before leaving it again on the right towards the valley. Some steps lead down to a bridge and a concrete track. We follow this up right. Above on the left is the cemetery chapel **2**. (For purists, the old monopáti runs for a few metres on the right). When the concrete track forks, you

0.30 head not towards the houses, but *left* up to the **helicopter landing site 3**. 40 m further on, you make your way right

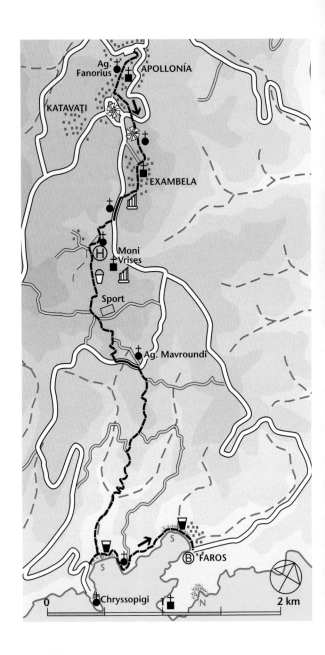

Ag.
Fanorius
APOLLONÍA

KATAVATI

EXAMBELA

Moni
Vrises

Sport

Ag. Mavroundi

B FAROS

0   2 km

Chryssopigi   N

towards the sea and into the realm of the monopátia. Another tower keeps watch on a hill to the left and the vast Monastery of St. Andrew resides above to the right . Some high walls on the right of the path guide us reliably ahead. We stroll on over pleasant paving stones, past a cistern with a nice place to sit. Heading down left at the

0.40 fork, you bear **right** towards the sea (blue dots) and not to the football ground. The church of Mavroundi then appears in a hollow on the left; we stay right at the fork ahead of it. Far below, the day's goal is already visible: the church of Chryssopigi on the rocky peninsula.

0.45 After quickly crossing the **road** on a slant, you wander up a farm track which forks after 130 m. Having turned right here, it is now hard to lose your way. You plunge into a maze of paths which all lead into the gorge. This widens towards the sea until we have reached our destination.

1.15 *The church of **Chryssopigi** (p. 173), which dates from 1650, lies on a peninsula and possesses a miracle-working icon. A steel model of a ship hangs above the altar. Future Greek seamen are baptised outside on the rocky peak, directly above the sea. A "place of strength".*

The way leads back to the beach, which is more attractive than that in Faros. If you're not ready to swim or sit and relax under the tamarisks of a taverna, stroll along the

1.35 wonderful coastal path, past a chapel, on to **Faros** . Here you can wait for the bus on the small beach or in a taverna at the water's edge.

㊸ The Way to Saint Simon

A trek of four to five hours through fields and valleys to the monastery of Agios Symeon, high above the bay of Kamarí. Easily identifiable paths offer fantastic views across the whole of Sífnos. Opportunities for bathing and eating wait at the end of the tour in Kamarí.

AWT 0.00 There is a stair-path from "Café Lakis" on the **square** of **Apollonía** leading up to Artemon/Artemónas. Up on the right is a large church with a blue dome **1** from where the path runs on to another hollow with a bridge. (Picnic items can be purchased in the supermarket to the right of the bridge). The steps of the skála lead uphill again to the elongated square of **Artemónas.** (You could consider the restaurant "Liotribi" for the evening!) Left of the ouzerie "Margerita", a lane continues straight on for about 150 m through fashionable Artemónas with its attractive gardens. You go left at a house straight in front of you. A few metres further ahead on the right is a church directly in the lane and, later on, the large church of Kochi with its blue dome on the left-hand side. You have to go down the gentle incline immediately on your left and then second right. Mt. Profitis Elias lies above to the left and the masts to the right as you leave the houses behind you. Some 350 m after the church of Kochi you reach the

0.20 **end of the village.** Here on the right is a metal signpost bearing today's destination: Agios Symeon! The path becomes more of an ideal monopáti at every step, cut away deeply in parts and lined with vines and olive trees **2**. It's more strolling than hiking. Though you should

0.30 not overlook the right-angled **left turn** where the metal sign is 10 m away from the fork! The view to the high mountain peak in the west **3**, atop which the white monastery of St. Simon awaits us, makes one slightly apprehensive at most. Though it's not as far as it looks. On the right in the middle of the fields is the Dimitri

★ Chapel **4** with a cistern. The mule track winds its way wonderfully through a hollow along a gentle downward slope

0.50 **5** to the large **cistern 6** hewn into the rocks to the right of the path. You go on a few steps down into the dry bed,

bearing right after 100 m to another modern cistern before climbing up a splendid stair-path **7**.

Unfortunately, the attractive steps turn into a scree path above, but our destination, Mt. Simon, has moved a good bit closer. Below the summit on the left is a telephone mast and, left of the path, you see (and smell) the ancient silver

1.10 mines of **Vorini** which are now filled in with rubbish. Here also begins the rather insensitively constructed roadway, built for the parish fair visitors who pilgrim here by car on 31st August every year. You alternate between the dirt track and the old pilgrims' way up to the summit.

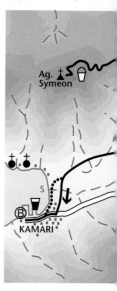

1.35 The monastery of **Agios Symeon** lies far removed, above the sea. As soon as you enter the courtyard, the view widens over the entire grounds down to the open, glittering sea **8**. It is a place of absolute silence. The windows allow you a glimpse through the church and to some long tables used to host the (mobile) pilgrims. Sitting on the monastery wall, you look down steeply into the fjord of Kamarí, our final goal. Time for a summit drink, if needs be from the faucet in the monastery courtyard. Further west is another monastery on a steep mountain:

Prof. Elias II which would take another 20 minutes to reach. Far out in the sea other Cycladic islands await us: Mílos with Kímolos and Sérifos.

But first we have to climb back down the mountain. As far as the mines of Vorini, the way to Kamarí is the same as on the way up.

> *The silver mines of **Vorini** are one of five ancient mines on Sífnos. In the 5th century BC, fettered slaves worked horizontally in the narrow tunnels, progressing 30 cm a day into the mountainside. The silver, which was minted in Aegina, made Sífnos the wealthiest Aegean island in antiquity.*

Ahead of the mine we bear right and stride down along the dirt road. A short cut is not possible as the terrain in between is too stony. Instead we do something for our fitness. Huge ruins dating from Venetian times draw closer and we enjoy the attractive view over the bay and the harbour.

The taverns lined up along the mole awaiting our arrival are already visible from above. Beforehand, we can jump into the water in the bay of **Kamarí.**

2.55

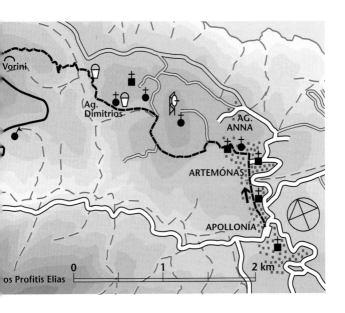

⑭ Above the Sea

This round tour of four to five hours (eight kms) leads through varied, agricultural landscape on the eastern side of the island, heading first along quiet Cycladic trails to Kastro, the former capital of the island. Then follows a longer stretch through superb terraces above the sea before continuing over a plateau back to Apollonía.

AWT 0.00   A lane, left of the raised site with the war memorial, leads from the **platía** in **Apollonía** into the maze of houses. We follow it for 50 m to a stair-path which leads down left and passes beneath the road. It is the paved track to the village of **Kato Petali**, which is soon visible on the hill opposite **❶**. Having come through a valley dotted with olive trees, past a bridge, you reach the village and pass to the right of

0.10   it. At the other end is a **large church** with a blue dome. Descending a few steps to the right, you go across a car park and head along a narrow concrete path on the other side to a sort of suburb. Here you proceed down a slight incline and then, opposite a chapel **❷**, left above the valley. After having passed a dovecote tower, you bear up left (red dots) at a fork onto a beautiful Cycladic trail. Soon you see

0.16   a **twin chapel** on the right, where you turn off left again. Then come two forks a short distance from each other: bear left at the first and right at the second! The xirolithíes are now metre-high on both sides. 50 m beyond a flat-roofed

0.20
0.25   **chapel** with a cistern to the right, you turn off right. Later on, the way will lead down left to the **road**.

> ▶ A dirt road leads up right from the bend to some attractive picnic and photo spots overlooking the former main village of the island **❸**.

Walk down 100 m along the road and, after the bend and the bridge, climb down a steep slope on the right onto a footpath marked with a green sign. A quiet chapel with a peaceful forecourt awaits us in the valley below. Heading down from here in the dry bed, scrambling at times, you

0.40   pass the cemetery and head up to **Kastro.** (If you want to jump into the water first, continue along the dry creek until you reach Serália, the harbour of Kastro, with a tiny beach and a taverna).

You should take your time to explore the listed village of Kastro and let yourself be carried along through the labyrinth of alleyways. The adjoining houses are built so as to form a fortress on the exterior, curving around the centre, with its narrow lanes and churches, by way of protection. From the vast ruins of the ancient acropolis, you look across to the next goal: a chapel and a church on the terraces above the sea **4**.

★

1.00
From the isthmus you wander below the windmill with the tin roof, at first on a dirt road, along the coast. At a right-hand bend, you climb up left a few metres and find a superb path which winds half way up the terraces, between two narrow walls above the sea. Contentedly, you arrive first at a chapel and then at **Panagia Poulati.** Below the church, directly on the path, you could find a Cycladic resting spot in a small, walled garden … Gentle terraces which you cannot tire of seeing lie between here and Kastro.

An odd signpost points in the direction of the old path which leads up the hill from the church. The picturesque, old stair-path **5** has recently been cut through in three places by a rough roadway. You can use the windmill of Artemónas as a bearing. The path ends on the flat above, in front of a house. Bearing right here, you soon see a superbly situated cemetery on the right. Below the village of Artemónas (two windmills), you turn right after a left-hand bend in the road onto a wall-lined track, then left uphill at a fork. Our monopáti takes us to the village higher up, which we can see to the north of the windmills. Below the village you have to cross a dusty road at an angle in

1.30
order reach **Agia Anna** up above.

Short cut: you go left at the hollow in Ag. Anna and reach Apollonía in 25 minutes via Artemónas.

The next stretch of the way leads up right between the houses. The hill with the aerial mast, at the foot of which is a cemetery, lies to the left. A wonderful, peaceful, panoramic way **6** leads north from here, high above the sea, following the contour lines. The wall on the left-hand side of the path is missing for a while. A steel water pipe has been laid next to the wall which reappears further on. The

1.45
path veers left, **heading inland**, and then forks. Turning left onto a dirt track, you bear left again where it forks in a southerly direction. You find yourself on a plateau with

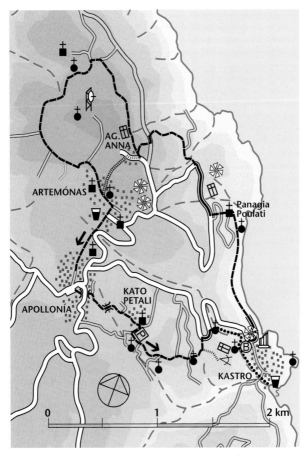

a monastery on the opposite slope above. Once again, who other than Prophet Elias keeps watch over it all! On our way between some field walls, we come past a chapel **7** then proceed straight ahead. The walls are higher here and, at a **fork** (on the right a metal sign to the Symeon Monastery in the opposite direction), you can already see Artemónas through the walls **8**. Now you only have to withstand the temptation of the two shady taverns on the elongated square of **Artemónas** in order to get back down safely to **Apollonía** over the steps of the wonderful skála.

2.00

2.10
2.20

Síkinos

Long off the beaten track, this island still lags a little behind its neighbours. There is no proper bus, and some room furnishings and the evening on the harbour are reminiscent of early visits to the Cyclades. It is bitter for the walker that the popular trail to Heróon has now been destroyed by a dirt road, without there being any obvious necessity.

㊺ From the Sea to the Source

The hike from Aloprónia takes us in roughly two hours up and down fairly steep slopes to the main settlement a twin village at an altitude of 270 m, before heading on to the white block of the monastery of Zoodóchos Pigís, the "life-giving source", above.

AWT

0.00   A dirt road beginning at the middle of the beach of **Aloprónia**, leads uphill from the electricity mast with a distribution box. Ignoring a left turn, you arrive at a deserted farmhouse at the top, 100 m in front of a church.

       Short cut: after the wall you can take a trail on the right (red dots) and thus shorten the route by 25 min.

0.20   The roadway leads to the locked **Church of Panagía** at a superb site above the bay of Aloprónia (fig.). From the apsis of the church it is easy to find the monopáti running uphill, which soon leads us through intensive green vegetation to a source and then into a wonderful rocky landscape. Here is another source. We cross a hollow and

0.45   proceed downhill along trails to the **ditch** where an unsealed road leads us right down to some olive trees. A short

0.55   while later, we take the **steps** up left on the other side of the valley, keeping *left* 80 m below the stone huts along the wide path over a rock, which then narrows to a monopáti leading over the ridge. A typical Greek landscape spreads before us: we cross a wide hollow with an olive grove and a defile, passing two cisterns before reaching a stairway which ends at the classicistic school building in

1.35 **Chóra.** There are two villages: up on the left, the younger Chorió (the village) and right, the part known as Kástro.

> *The **Kástro**, the fortress like settlement, which once stood on what is now the flat main square, was torn down during the Italian occupation. Small alleys invite you to take a stroll; a suitable tavern is also to be found.*

To find a spectacular picnic spot, climb up the white-washed steps up to the abandoned, fortress-like convent

1.45 of **Zoodóchos Pigís**, perched on a steep cliff. You have an eagle's eye view, far across the Cyclades.

Unfortunately, the new roadway to Heróon / Episkopí is also visible to the right of Chorió. It has been built with unbelievable insensitivity, burying the old trail, formerly one of the most popular hiking trails on the Cyclades, beneath it. An eight to ten metre-wide track has been ploughed through the terrain. The art-historical goal at the end of the track – the huge Roman tomb, or Heróon, which was later converted into the church of Episkopí – is now no longer accessible. Anyone still wanting to visit the peaceful area around the tomb, will need an hour along the unsealed road. Scouts can use the remains of some old paths which run parallel below the road.

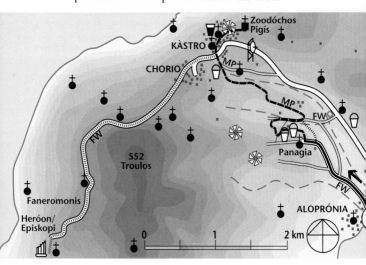

Síros

A marble mountain crest forms the backbone of the island. To the south there are wide, green valleys, whereas the north is partially barren. Apart from its beautiful sandy bays and some lonely mule tracks, the elegant, non-touristic capital Ermoupolis displays big city Mediterranean flair.

Plati Vouni

Pirgos

Kiní

Ano Syros

Ermoúpolis

Agía Varváras

Gallissás

Fínikas

Chroúsa

Vári

Posidonía

㊻ Síros – Not Just a Stopover

Síros is one of the main seaports on the Cyclades. A day's stopover can well be used for this trek. This round tour of five hours heads over karst-type landscape and cultivated terraces and also leads us through the alleys and stairways of Ermoúpolis to the two dominating churches. Long trousers are recommended for this hike!

AWT 0.00   Taking the stairway left of the neo-classical town hall on **Miauli Square** in **Ermoúpolis**, you turn left at the turning after the steps and use the staircase leading up at an angle. Then heading up port side (right) from the "bows" with the figurehead **1**, you bear left at the end of the beautiful stairway. 70 m further on, you come across a wide stair-path along which you bear right and then straight ahead in the direction of Ano Síros. Having turned left where the

0.10   road forks, you ascend the steps, cross the **asphalt road** and head left, up and down the steps, halfway up the slope of the mountain on which the town is built.

> *Ano Síros, the Catholic quarter, is built in the Cycladic style, in contrast to the newer, lower part of the town, and is dominated by the Cathedral of St. George.*

0.25   On the west side of the last bend of a serpentine road, a **paved way 2** leads below a chapel into a gorge.

> *Alternative:* **after heavy rains** it is better to turn up right 50 m further on, then left straight after, using the road for 600 m.

Otherwise you continue straight ahead over some lovely paving stones, turning down left ahead of the monastery into the dry bed where worn paths **3** lead through the gorge. You bear up right ahead of the wall at the end of the valley, then left along a short stretch of road before heading through a small hollow without a path. On the other side you climb up over bedrock and an overgrown

1.00   footpath to a chapel, then come to the village of **Mitaki** via the road. Turning right at the fork, you follow a wide left bend of the road around a broad, at times elaborately terraced valley **4**.

1.25   *Ahead* of the **chapel of St. George** at the fork in the road, you branch off down right over open ground. On the left

	below, a footpath leaves the village of **Plati Vouri** . We
1.40	try to **reach** it half way up, from where it leads us right in
	a southerly direction. Later on, above the path are two
1.55	**caves** with a terrace where the philosopher Ferekides,

below, a footpath leaves the village of **Plati Vouri** 🄵. We
1.40 try to **reach** it half way up, from where it leads us right in
a southerly direction. Later on, above the path are two
1.55 **caves** with a terrace where the philosopher Ferekides,
Pythagoras' teacher, is said to have held classes. The way
🄶 becomes somewhat overgrown but can still be easily
identified. Both the wide view across to Tínos, Mykonos,
Naxos and Paros and the scent of thyme entice you to
linger. Up in the hamlet of Richipo, you wander past a
2.10 **group of houses** (left), heading straight onto a monopáti
which runs left past the next hilltop and soon offers a wide
panoramic view of Ermoúpolis, with the steep slope of
Ano Síros and the vast block of the church of St. George
🄷. The path becomes rather prickly and narrow on the way
down and leads on left below, past two hills, towards the
blue dome of the Anastasia Cathedral.
2.45 You head right along the **asphalt road** to where the road
widens on the left. 50 m further on, a wide skála leads
down to the left. This is Ermoúpolis! The best view is from
the cathedral above.
The stairway leads straight down and around the church
of St. Nikolaos, heading on towards the **town bathing**
3.00 **area** with a taverna 🄸. The AWT ends here …

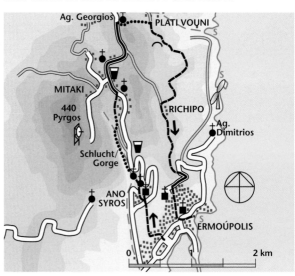

Tínos

The diverse landscape with marble, granite and schist mountains and fertile, green valley floors is ideally suited for hiking tours. The island, which was "canonized" in 1971, still has numerous beautiful monopátia along which one encounters the famous, artistically decorated dovecotes, relics of the Venetian domination of the Cyclades.

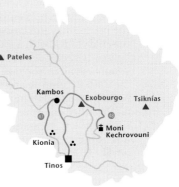

ⓐ La Paloma

In three to four hours you wander past the most attractive dovecote towers on Tínos to the sea. Orientation along the mule tracks is easy; there are cisterns en route and some good taverns on the beach.

AWT 0.00   Having got off at the bus stop of **Tarampados** and walked down into the village, you soon see the dovecote towers, the symbols of Tínos, on the other side of the slope. About ten of the most attractive are built here in the gardens!

Ten metres ahead of the blue sign, you head down left along a lane into the valley and turn left before a small church **1** onto a paved path. This is cut away deeply in places so that it is hard to see all the **dovecote towers 2 3**.

> *The Venetians, who had a particular liking for dove meat and eggs, were the first to build towers for rearing pigeons. Marinated dove was later exported to the whole of the Aegean. The pigeons also carried messages and provided dung. There are 1300 of the two-storeyed dovecote towers on Tínos.*
>
> *You can traverse the valley on several narrow paths and take a closer look at the elaborate, triangular-shaped decorations.*

There is a well next to some washing troughs in a cavern to the left of the path, which later becomes a dry bed. You

0.10   head up to the left where it widens to form a **triangle.** On the left – a few hundredths of a second for the photographers: dovecote towers pure. The road crosses our path further on. On the other side, you head along a dirt track for a short stretch, then continue without a path towards the power lines and cross some dry-stone walls to a twin-towered church with a tiled roof **4**. The huge crag of Exobourgo is visible on the left and the convent of Kechrovouni beyond it. You take the mule track down left before

0.20   the Catholic **church** and head up right immediately after, passing around the church. There is a dirt track on the left on the other side which becomes a mule track after 30 m. Up on the left is a house with a chapel. You bear left at the fork along a rocky mule track which leads downhill later on **5**. At a right bend (marking), Delos and Mykonos

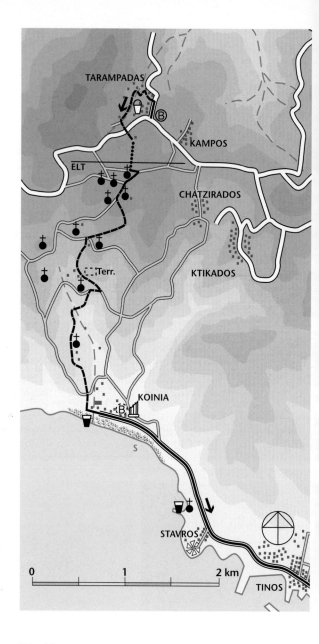

TARAMPADAS

KAMPOS

ELT

CHATZIRADOS

Terr.

KTIKADOS

KOINIA

S

STAVROS

TINOS

0   1   2 km

0.35   appear ahead. Where the **way forks** at some ruins, the wider track leads us right down some steps (red arrows). A few metres further on, we turn off left. Having gone around

0.45   the hill, a **large terrace** appears on the left of the track and some stables and a threshing circle on the right. On the other side of the lush, green valley you see a chapel and, below, the bay of Kionia with a rather oversized hotel. You follow the track around the terrace and on downhill through an olive grove. Further down the slope, you walk right for 100 m towards the chapel **6**, but climb down left *before* you reach it, over a rather overgrown track into a

1.00   quiet, reed-lined **creek.** 20 m upstream is a pool in the rocks which is full in spring!

Some steps lead up the other side of the dry bed and more dovecote towers are visible in the olive groves on the left below. Walking right between a few dilapidated stables, you bear right above a chapel **7**, then right again, staying above the olive trees. A short dirt road leads to the green,

1.20   **sandy beach of Kiona 8**. Here you can swim, arrange pebbles according to colour, have a good meal or (until 3 p.m.) visit some ancient ruins.

> *Little is left of the **Poseidon Shrine** (an almost 3000-year old spa and medicinal bath) since part of it was used to build the pilgrimage church of Tínos (1830!). The loose arrangement of the surviving remains demonstrates that the Greeks must already have detested aligning axes back then. It is a beautiful site well worth a visit.*

Only in summer are there busses to Tínos. At other times you can either ask the driver of one of the frequently empty taxis how much it will cost, hitchhike back or set

1.55   off along the fairly quiet road to **Tínos town on foot,** passing Stavros en route where a heavenly café has set up in a church building next to the beach. A place to enjoy the evening sun.

What the weather's like at home?

㊽ Exobourgo

The six-hour trek begins after a visit to the convent and leads around the mighty crag of Exobourgo, where a huge Venetian fortress once stood. The tour can be split into two parts, either taking the bus from Kampos or hiking directly to Tínos from Exobourgo. There is a taverna after three and a half hours.

The **bus** to Steni/Monasteri brings you to the **Convent of Kechrovouni** up on the mountain.

> *Numerous nuns live in shared accommodation in the convent village. Next to the upper church is the cell of Pelagía, the nun, whose vision of the famous icon of the Virgin Mary led to the present renown (and wealth) of Tínos. The icon was discovered by chance in 1823 which greatly aided the Greek uprising against the Turks.*
> *The destination of the trek, the rock of Exobourgo* ■, *is visible above the roofs of the convent.*

AWT 0.00 Having come **out of the convent**, you go 200 m right to the crossing and then right again from there. Some 600 m along the road, an overgrown monopáti ■ comes up on

0.08 the left. Here you **leave the road** and fight your way through the bushes. Approximately 100 m further on, after a wire fence, the path clears again. Arriving at a dilapidated dovecote and a chapel (on the right), you bear left downhill, either on or alongside the overgrown path, to another chapel. There is a sea of flowers here in the spring! You head right below the chapel, through a hollow with a spring, then uphill turning left at the fork, following the contour lines directly on the wall and, shortly before the village of **Karyá**, through another dry bed.

0.25 Opposite the **church** (on the right) you proceed horizontally, past a well, through the village along to the church on the right-hand side, taking the concrete track up right – to yet another church above the village. Behind it stretches a quiet track with places to rest and an attractive view. It leads on to a chapel with a house (left),

0.40 then through a hollow and a dry bed up to the **road**, which you follow left ■. Left and right are the cisterns of the destroyed Venetian town. On the way up to the

immense mountain fortress, you pass the ruins of a palace on the left of the road.

> *The ascent of the 540 m-high **Exobourgo** will take an additional ten minutes. The Venetian defensive installations were immediately razed by the Ottomans after being surrendered without a fight in 1715. Thus practically all that remains here today is the fantastic view of the Aegean.*

Anyone wanting to enjoy it a while longer, can **cut short** the rest of the tour by two hours: on the mountain below is a stair-path which leads to Trípotamos and Tínos (see map: ABK).

0.50 Back at the foot of the mountain, you bear north ahead of the two **churches**, one of which is Roman Catholic. In the valley below lies the village of Kumaros, to which we climb down left over a paved track after a right bend in the road (from a stable with a forecourt). 20 m before reaching the first archway with a kafeníon, you head left down some steps and then immediately left again. We come onto a charming, shady path. The steep, rather narrow way leads under fig trees and oaks into the valley. From a creek bed

1.20 you bear left onto a flat dirt track along to the **road** (bus stop).

After having crossed it, you go right downhill into **Loytra** and then down to the right before the garden gate to the Catholic Ursuline convent. You bear left in the village to the Jesuit monastery/museum. There is a well in front of the museum.

1.25 Passing the **square** in front of the Jesuit church on your right, you go straight on over the roadway onto the narrow way leading downhill from the red markings (arrow 3). Kampos, with its blue-domed church, waits up at the end of the valley.

The wonderful trail through the fields **4** leads uphill again at a dry bed to an ancient olive grove with a dovecote. At some ruins, you wander up right (red markings), continuing along a romantic oak-lined trail. Bearing left at the fork, you continue straight after through a dry creek, at the end of which some steps lead up left (at times through the undergrowth). At the top you turn right and then further down, before the village, up left to a dirt track. You head left here, continue later on a footpath to the right, then

2.00 without a trail past a windmill to the **road**.

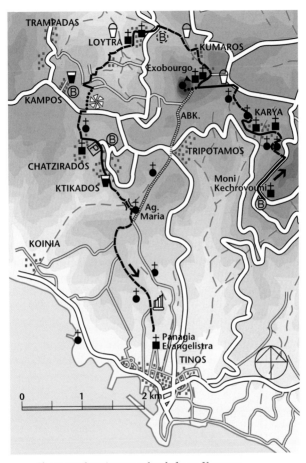

Short cut: bus journey back from Kampos.

Otherwise you walk 20 m right along the road, turning off
left at the blue signpost. We then disappear between dry-
stone walls onto an attractive path **5**. *Below* the chapel on
2.10   the wayside, you descend to **Chatzirados.** Heading around
the upper edge of the village, you climb down the steps
below the car park at the other end. Then pass some
washing troughs in a hollow and along a passageway
through a house. At the end of the village you turn right
(towards the windmill), hiking along the road into pic-

turesque **Ktikados** (bus connection!). The superb taverna
2.20 "Drosia" 🅖 awaits us at the other end. Sat in the shade
(=gr.: "drosia") on the terrace, enjoying the view to the sea,
you draw your breath for the last leg. The way ahead must
also be enjoyed!

You head down right from the tavern towards the end of
the village. Here, on the left, begins the narrow, initially
rather overgrown path which leads along the slope above
the valley. St. Mary's chapel 🅗 is already visible on the
★ opposite slope. But first we descend into the valley and
2.35 pilgrim over some wonderful steps up to the **chapel**.
Ahead of us, a visual treat: the Cycladic perfection of
Mykonos and Delos in the deep blue Aegean! Ahead of the
chapel, we take the paved path to the right. It was built by
the Venetians in the Middle Ages as a link from the harbour
to Exobourgo. They withdrew this way under the escort of
the Ottomans in 1715, leaving the Cyclades for good.
Venetian rule of the Cyclades ended here. Guilty of
treason, the last commanding officer ended up in the
dungeons.

Our descent here this evening is far more pleasant 🅘.
Coming past the remains of a Dionysus temple, we arrive
3.10 in the upper part of **Tínos**, after having walked 12 km.

Backpacker's Paperbacks
Bookstores with foreign books

Amorgós, Katápola
→ *Peppas* (books and fax service)
→ *Simona* (Hairdressers and
second-hand books) next to
Moon Café, Xilokeratidi
Andros, Chora → *Laleon books*
Folégandros, Chóra → Loan of
books in the taverna on the
first square after the bus station
Milos, Adamas → *Mourilis books*
Adamandas Milou
Mykonos, Chóra→ *News Stand*
5 Kabani Road, parallel to the
harbour road
Naxos, Chóra → *Zoom* on the
harbour road
→ *Vrakas* (Gold and second-
hand books), harbour road

Paros, Parikia → *Bizas bookstore*
market street
→ *Spyridis books* La Palma
→ *Sailing* (General goods and
second-hand books), harbour
road
Santoríni, Thíra → *Euro books*
Central Square, **Kamári** → *Kali-Bazaar* (Clothes and second-
hand books) Side road off the
promenade
Sífnos, Kamári → *Bookshop* on
the harbour
Síros, Port → *Asmanis books*
Akti Petrou Rali
Tínos, Chora → *Krikelis books*
Paralia Tinou 11

Abbreviations, Key

———	hiking route on a roadway
– – – –	hiking route on a path
••••••••	hiking route without a path
ALT/ABK ıııııııııı	alternative route / short cut
– –	dry streambed (at times), hollow
←	direction of route
⚐	antennae
⚑ ⚐	Venetian fortress / dwelling tower / ruins
Ⓑ	bus stop
FW	unclassified road / dirt track
⊞	cemetery
Ⓗ	helicopter landing pad
⛪	monastery / large church
⛪ ⛪	chapel / summit church
⥿	marker post
MP	monopáti / mule track
N	nude bathing possible
🏛	ancient ruins
S	beach
ST	street
Ⓣ	petrol station
▼	tavern
ℙ	car park
✳	windmill / torso
⌘	cistern / well / spring
⌒	cave
★	The author's 15 favourite spots

Help! Please notify us if you discover that the situation has changed. Perhaps I will be able to assist you with a hotel tip from my wanderings on the island you're headed for.

Graf Editions
Elisabethstr. 29, 80796 München, Germany
Tel. 0049-89-271 59 57, Fax 0049-89-271 59 97

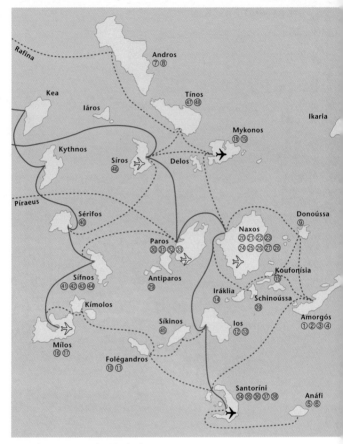

Travel routes on the Cyclades

✈ International airport

✈ (small) Domestic airport

— Frequently-used shipping route

· · · · Infrequently-used shipping route

㊽ Walking tour

100 metres = 109 yards
1 kilometre = 0,63 miles
1 mile = 1,6 kilometres
100 yards = 91,5 metres